Interrogating Privilege:
Reflections of a Second Language Educator

STEPHANIE VANDRICK

To Elaine,
with best wishes and
with happy memories of our
Nodai days!
Stephanie

Ann Arbor
University of Michigan Press

To my family, who mean everything to me:
Jahan, Mariam, Norrie, Ken, Ian, Paul, Marilyn, Joyce, Eric,
Allison, Jessica, Chiara, Priya, Giselle, Andrew, and Levi

Copyright © by Stephanie Vandrick 2009
Published in the United States of America
The University of Michigan Press
Manufactured in the United States of America

∞ Printed on acid-free paper

ISBN-13: 978-0-472-03394-2

2012   2011   2010   2009   4   3   2   1

Library of Congress Cataloging-in-Publication Data

Vandrick, Stephanie.
    Interrogating privilege : reflections of a second language
educator / Stephanie Vandrick.
        p. cm.
    Includes bibliographical references and index.
    ISBN 978-0-472-03394-2 (pbk. : alk. paper)
    1. Vandrick, Stephanie. 2. English teachers—United States—
Biography. 3. Women college teachers—United States—Biography. 4.
English language—Study and teaching—Foreign speakers. 5. Second
language acquisition. I. Title.
    PE64.V35A3 2009
    428.0092—dc22
    [B]   2009033222

Preface

In a recent semester, I had what I would consider a "perfect class," in which the interesting and interested students, great materials and discussions, comfortable and light-filled classroom, and general sense of well being combined to remind me of how fortunate I am to be able to teach such classes and such students. It also reminded me of the types of privilege that both the students and I possess, privilege that allows for such a fulfilling educational experience. The students have time and money, I have a reasonable schedule and workload, the university provides an intellectually rich atmosphere, and we are located on a lovely, green, safe campus in a beautiful, multicultural, progressive city. I know that my students and I are fortunate; I am also very aware that many students and instructors are less fortunate. The lens of privilege through which I examined the experience of teaching my "perfect class" is the lens through which I examine my—and by extension, that of other ESOL educators'—teaching and scholarly work and environment in this book.

In this book, I explore privilege in its various forms in second language education, and in particular in university-level ESOL teaching. I do so through a hybrid form: a blend of traditional academic research/writing and personal narrative. My aim is to observe and address the experiences of teachers/scholars and students as "whole persons," and to look at all the identities and issues that participants in the educational process bring with them to the educational site. I believe that we too often focus only on class syllabi, objectives, and materials, and on learning processes—all, of course, very important—but don't give enough attention to the various identities and various types of privilege, or lack of privilege, that each individual brings to the educational setting. Thus the chapters in this book not only address some specifics of the classroom and of pedagogy, but also take a wider-angled look at the educational process, its sites, its participants, their identities, and how these elements interact in various ways.

Each chapter has a different focus, and can be read as a stand-alone piece, but the chapters also interact with each other. Some chapters are longer, some shorter; some have more traditional academic features (more references, for example) and others are more narrative-oriented and essayistic, depending on the topic and on my experiences related to that topic.

The stories are all true, although in most cases names and identifying details have been changed to protect the confidentiality of students, colleagues, and others.

This book is the culmination of my many years of reading, thinking, and writing, both about the teaching life and about the wider life of educators. In addition to referring to TESOL and applied linguistics sources, I bring to this book my reading, experiences, and interests in the areas of pedagogy, writing, literature, psychology, culture, feminism, identities, politics, postmodernism, postcolonialism, travel, community, and more. I hope that I have been able to weave these many strands together in a way that enriches the conversation in TESOL, and sheds some light on the experiences that those of us in second language education, especially in TESOL, experience. Further, although the majority of my teaching experience is in TESOL, I hope that many of the topics I discuss and the experiences I describe will resonate with other educators as well.

Acknowledgments

I owe gratitude to so many people who inspired, supported, and encouraged me before and during the writing of this book: my colleagues, friends, students, editor, and family.

At the University of San Francisco (USF), where I teach, the members of my writing group—Bernadette Barker-Plummer, Karen Bouwer, and Kathy Nasstrom—have helped me more than words can say, liberally providing advice, strategies, encouragement when things are not going well, and celebrations when they are. The Friday "Writing Warriors" of the College of Arts and Sciences at USF have also helped to keep me writing, providing a structured writing setting as well as collegiality and good humor; special thanks go to Tracy Seeley, who organized the Friday writing days on campus. Many thanks, too, go to Dean Jennifer Turpin, who supports the Friday writing days, and supports as well the weekend writing retreats in the College of Arts and Sciences at USF; one writing weekend in Spring 2006 was particularly helpful in jump-starting my writing of this book. For many years of active support, sometimes during very difficult times, my deep gratitude goes to Johnnie Johnson Hafernik, the late Shigeo Imamura, Michael Lehmann, and Stanley Nel, four people at USF whose influence and assistance have been critically, even essentially, important to me and my career.

I am fortunate to have many close colleagues and friends in the TESOL world, all of whom have, in various ways, influenced me and my work, including this book. First, heartfelt thanks are due to Christine Pearson Casanave, with whom I have an ongoing conversation about scholarship and writing, and who gives me excellent editing advice. She read every chapter of this book and gave me extremely useful feedback; in addition, she suggested the title of this book. I also thank a wonderful group that I am very lucky to be part of: the Sister Scholars, consisting of Rachel Grant, Ryuko Kubota, Angel Lin, Suhanthie Motha, Gertrude Tinker-Sachs, and Shelley Wong; together we have created a unique community and lasting friendships that I treasure. For generous inspiration, conversation, and friendship, I particularly and deeply appreciate two TESOL colleagues and friends, Sarah Benesch and Brian Morgan. Other colleagues and friends in the TESOL world who have also enriched my intellectual, academic, and personal lives with joint projects and conversations, and with their friendship, include Dwight Atkinson, Diane Belcher, Linda Lonon Blanton, Suresh Canagarajah, Christian Chun, Graham Crookes, Sonja Franeta, Adrian Holliday, Bill Johnston, Rick Kappra, Ena Lee, Ilona Leki, Aya Matsuda, Paul Kei Matsuda, Dorothy Messerschmitt, Bonny Norton, Alastair Pennycook, Matthew Prior, Vaidehi Ramanathan, Ruth Spack, and Sue Starfield.

In my life outside academe, I have been blessed in my friendships, including those with the members of two groups that have provided friendship and memorable gatherings for many years: my Reading Group, which has been meeting for over thirty years, includes Marcy Jackson, Kathy King, Martha Lynch, Janet McColl, and Helen Munch; my Mothers' Group, which has been meeting for twenty years, consists of Phyllis Cath, Lynne Schuman, and Ianthia Hall Smith. I cherish my long, sustaining friendship with my dear friend Mary Cox Valle. I especially thank my close friend Connie O'Keefe, with whom I have had countless wonderful conversations about reading, writing, and life throughout the many years since we were in graduate school together.

Teaching is the heart of my academic work, and I thank the students who have taken my classes, in particular the students whose stories appear in this book, especially "Valerie."

I thank University of Michigan Press editor Kelly Sippell for being receptive to this book despite its not fitting easily into any obvious academic genre or category, and for understanding what I am attempting to do here; I truly appreciate the support and guidance she has provided me as I have worked on this book. I appreciate as well the work of the various University of Michigan Press reviewers, editors, and designers who helped to make this book a reality. I also thank Bernadette Pedagno, a USF colleague who kindly proofread the manuscript and assisted me with other editorial matters.

All my life, I have been sustained by my wonderful family, and I thank them with all my heart for their unfailing, unconditional love and support: my husband Jahan Missaghi and daughter Mariam Missaghi, my mother Norrie Vandrick and late father John Vandrick, and my brothers Ken, Ian, and Paul and their families.

Finally, as this book is about privilege, I want to acknowledge the invaluable and much-appreciated privilege that I have as an academic, the privilege that has allowed me to spend my life teaching, reading, thinking, researching, and writing, and that has allowed me to write this book.

Contents

Chapter 1

An Introduction

I am writing a book of personal essays that I hope will illuminate issues related to privilege in education, especially second language education, in particular TESOL. These chapters contain stories about myself, about my students, about my colleagues, and about academe, in the context of our larger society. The chapters follow a different path than most academic writing; they blend theory, analysis, and narrative. I hope that readers will find the essays both engaging and thought-provoking.

Yet as I begin writing the introductory chapter—this one—I find myself writing in generalizations and in academic-speak. I need to do so in order to explain the book to readers, especially, first, on the topic of privilege and, second, on my reasons for the choice I have made to write very personally. So I am caught in a contradiction: I seem to need to write in a somewhat traditional academic style in this introduction before getting to the chapters that combine academic analysis with personal narratives.

I begin each chapter with a story or a note; in the case of
this introductory chapter, I begin instead with this appeal
to you, the reader, to understand my dilemma, and to read
this chapter for background, as a foundation for the rest
of the book, with the understanding that you will soon
get to the main text, the body of the book: my narrative
essays.

A look around any classroom, including any ESOL classroom, will
show how many identities students and instructors have. Various
nationalities, ethnicities, races, social classes, genders, sexual orientations,
religions, abilities, disabilities, health statuses, and ages are among the
identities on display, or sometimes hidden but still important, in classrooms. Privilege and its effects are found everywhere, in and out of
classrooms, yet privilege is often invisible, and even when it is visible, we
often prefer not to acknowledge it. In the United States, we like to think
that everyone has equal opportunities to succeed if she or he is willing
to work hard. Many in the United States and elsewhere, including those
of us in academe, seem to be made uncomfortable by the thought that
privilege is so prevalent, and so powerful in its effects on people's lives.
In particular, we seem not to want to talk about social class privilege;
however, class privilege is extremely powerful, both on its own and in its
interactions with other identities such as gender, race, and sexual identity.
As bell hooks so forcefully puts it, "As a nation we are afraid to have a
dialogue about class even though the ever-widening gap between rich
and poor has already set the stage for ongoing and sustained class war-
fare" (2000b, p. 11). Proweller (1998) adds that

> While class is a central category of social analysis
> inside American culture and society, it remains a
> relatively unspoken descriptor, commonly filtered
> through discourses of gender, race, and ethnicity.

> The "myth of classlessness" is notable among
> Americans in general who tend to describe them-
> selves as middle class because they see the middle
> class as a *universal class* with *universal* member-
> ship. (p. 69)

Although educators tend to be progressive, and are perhaps more aware of certain types of privilege (such as racial privilege) than others, there is still a tendency not to want to acknowledge the profound effects of privilege, or lack thereof.

In this book, I explore the following topics as they relate to education, especially second language education/TESOL: which identities are privileged; when, how, and why they are privileged; how these identities, including their accompanying privileges or lack thereof, intersect and interact; ways in which identities are not unified or static, but rather multiple and fluid and evolving; and what the effects of such varying types and levels of privilege are in the classrooms, institutions, and societies in which we teach and live. My own teaching site is a university in the United States, and most of my stories and my examinations of privilege are in that context, but I believe that they also have a wider resonance.

As I discuss various types of privilege that do or do not accompany various identities, I hope it will be clear that I am not "judging" any of these identities as inherently better or worse; rather, I am attempting to identify these identities, especially as they exist in the ESOL world and, more generally, in the world of education, and to examine ways in which privilege manifests itself and makes its influence felt. In addition, I am hoping that such examination will facilitate both instructors' and students' taking responsibility for acknowledging their (our) privilege and its ramifications in our educational settings.

Note that throughout this book I use the terms ESOL and ESL interchangeably. ESL is still the most widely used term, and thus more widely recognized; ESOL is more accurate, in that for many students, English is not simply a second language but perhaps a third or fourth language, and may be used equally with a first language, or may only be used in certain contexts and for certain specific purposes. I use the term TESOL when I refer to the teaching aspect of our work, but also in a larger sense when I refer to our profession and our academic field.

This introductory chapter is divided into three sections. In the first, I discuss social class, as it is the identity I most focus on in this book, along with its intersections with other identities and other forms of privilege. In the second section, I explore the role of personal narrative in scholarly writing, and I discuss my reasons for choosing to write in a hybrid genre that blends personal narrative with more traditional academic writing. In the third section, I provide an overview of the structure of the book.

Social Class in Interaction with Other Types of Privilege

I am concerned about and interested in all types of privilege and their manifestations, especially in ESOL classrooms and environs, and in this book I examine privilege related to gender, race, sexual identity, academic status, age, and other identities and factors. In particular, the strongest focus of this book is on one specific aspect of privilege: the social class identities of ESOL students and their instructors, and the effects of social class privilege on students, faculty, and educational institutions. Even when addressing other factors, such as gender or sexual identity, I look at the connections and interactions between those identities and social class identities. One reason for this focus is that social class status is even less acknowledged than many other identities. In our professional literature, and even in our classrooms, ESOL educators have increasingly—although still not enough—discussed race and gender, but very rarely discuss class. And in the few instances when ESOL scholars address class issues (e.g., Auerbach, 1993; Auerbach & Burgess, 1985; Benesch, 2001; Morgan, 1998), they almost always focus on working-class or poor students. Middle-class identities are almost never addressed, perhaps because middle class is considered the norm and therefore an unmarked identity. Upper-class identities are even less often addressed. Because of this near universal lack of mention of the middle and upper classes, and because many of the students in my university classes, at an expensive private university, come with a great deal of social class privilege, this is a topic I have explored in my own work, especially in an article entitled "Privileged ESL University Students" (Vandrick, 1995a). In that article, I noted the signs of privilege displayed by wealthy international students, such as expensive cars and clothing, and often attitudes of entitlement, and I noted that such privilege affected the dynamics of the classroom. Less privileged students sometimes feel inferior and/or resentful; even instructors may feel resentful, especially if they feel they are being treated as glorified servants. I have also studied a subset of this privileged group, one I call "students of the new global elite" (Vandrick, 2007); these students are not only wealthy and privileged, but have lived and studied in at least three countries. They are "a curious combination of rooted and untethered; they are rooted in one place, yet they have acquired additional roots elsewhere; they feel comfortable and connected everywhere and yet do not feel they totally belong anywhere" (Vandrick, 2007). Although it is probably true that students with these identities are—by virtue of the very class privilege they enjoy—less in need of understanding and aid than others, I believe that it is important to examine all levels of social class identity, to provide a full picture, and to see how each level affects and is affected by our instruction and classroom interactions.

There are more publications about social class in our "sister" field, composition studies, as well as in English studies and related fields, but not many. Curiously, the biggest single group of publications about social class in composition studies seems to be edited collections of essays by working-class academics about their own experiences in academe, such as those by Shepard, McMillan, and Tate (1998), Tokarczyk and Fay (1993), and Zandy (1994). Those who have written about the class status of students (occasionally referring to the class status of faculty as well) include Coiner, Frankenstein, Miller, Rudnick, and Slapikoff (1995); hooks (2000a, 2000b); Ohmann (2003); and Tate (1997). Again, writings about the middle or upper classes, whether referring to students or faculty, are much rarer. Bloom's article "Freshman Composition as a Middle-Class Enterprise" (1996) is one well-known exception; another exception is Proweller's (1998) research on upper middle-class youth culture.

Academe itself is classed. Certain universities—especially certain private universities—have more prestige than other institutions. Research universities have more prestige than others. Universities with graduate programs generally have more status than those without, and both have more status than community or junior colleges. Faculty, too, are definitely classed: In addition to possessing the status provided by various professorial ranks, those with tenure are regarded more highly than those without, and those with full-time jobs have much more status than those with part-time positions. Students with higher social class levels are more likely to attend institutions with higher statuses. Each reinforces the other. Universities benefit from students who can pay full (high) tuition and who are often better prepared because of their access to good schools and resources during their elementary and high school years; students benefit from the high status of the more prestigious universities because they gain a reflected high status from their attendance there, and because their degrees from such institutions often help them attain more success after college (DeGenaro, 2001; Soliday, 1999). O'Dair (2003) notes that although higher education has expanded, affluent students make up a higher proportion of undergraduates now than in the past. Thus institutions themselves both empower and reproduce class differences (Bourdieu & Passeron, 1977).

These are not just matters of graduation and career statistics. These are matters of the lived experiences of students and instructors being strongly affected by their social class identities. Sternglass (1997), among others, reminds us that just paying for college and earning degrees within a reasonable number of years are highly classed activities; she quotes one student, Ricardo, saying "I've been on the honor roll for three years, but if I can't pay the rent and eat, who cares about grades?" (p. 105). Bell hooks (2000a) tells us, with her strong feelings still evident many years after the fact, of her difficult experiences as a young student from an African-American working-class family attending Stanford University. She speaks of students who "flaunted their wealth and family background" (n.p.) and who trashed her room as a prank:

> I hated that girls who had so much, took so much
> for granted, never considered that those of us
> who did not have mad money would not be able
> to replace broken things . . . that we did not
> know everything could be taken care of at the dry
> cleaner's, because we never took our clothes there.
> (n.p.)

The social class split may be most obvious at elite universities such as Stanford, but almost every university has students (and faculty) from a range of class and economic backgrounds, and there are often tensions between those at the two ends of the continuum. International undergraduate students are generally at the higher end of the class spectrum, as they almost always have to be able to pay full tuition (as opposed to immigrant students, who often have legal resident or citizen status, and thus pay in-state tuition at state universities; immigrant students are also eligible for financial aid). For example, at the private university where I teach, my students "write unself-consciously of their parents in high positions, of summer homes, of expensive overseas vacations, of servants, of parties at exclusive hotels and clubs, and of upscale cars given them on their sixteenth birthdays" (Vandrick, 1995a, p. 375). In addition to the obvious material manifestations of wealth, these students generally exhibit "the self-assured, comfortable demeanor usually found among young people who are used to financial security and privilege"; there is also often "a clear sense of entitlement, of feeling that it [is] natural and given that they [are] among the affluent and elite" (Vandrick, 2007, n.p.).

One whole area of emphasis and concern that is clearly underpinned by class differences is the area of remediation and accompanying perceptions of deficit. Many students who are labeled as "underprepared" (and this label often has to do with language skills) and needing remediation, before or while being mainstreamed, are from social class backgrounds that did not provide them adequate educational preparation for higher education, and these are concerns that should be addressed. However, remediation has sometimes become a way to separate (some would say ghettoize) students from such backgrounds from more prosperous students from middle- and upper-class backgrounds. There is much discussion in academe, and in particularly in writing programs, about how best to deal with such differences in preparation. Should there be separate sections of composition for underprepared students? Should students who come from immigrant families and whose English language abilities may still not be on a par with those of native speakers be in separate sections? (For more detailed discussion of such issues of remediation, see Benesch, 1988, 1991; Merisotis & Phipps, 2000; Soliday, 2002.)

As for faculty—who were once students as well—one of the most heart-wrenching stories I have read in an academic publication is that of Patricia A. Sullivan, a long-time and well-established professor of composition. Sullivan came from a very deprived working-class background, and for years she never told anyone about this background; she excelled at "passing" as middle class. But at a certain point she came to feel it was wrong that "Class is academe's dirty little secret, its last taboo, that about which we dare not speak" (1998, p. 239), and she decided, with much trepidation, to speak out about her own background. She writes of working sixteen-hour shifts, living in the cheapest dorm, receiving smuggled-from-the-cafeteria food from friends, getting food stamps, doing without new clothes or shoes, and borrowing toothpaste and shampoo from her roommate. Other working-class academics describe how difficult it was

> to picture themselves as being academics, how little support they received, how they felt unen- titled, and felt that others from the middle and upper classes knew the secrets of academe, which they, shamefully, did not. They speak of passing, of anger, of loneliness. (Vandrick, 2001a, p. 28)

Sometimes these class differences not only cause mental and emotional anguish for faculty, but can actually be a source of (generally unintentional) discrimination. Some years ago I became familiar with a situation in which an applicant for an academic job, though in many ways the most qualified candidate, was not chosen for the position. It seemed to me that the main reason she was not chosen was certain "markers" which indicated that she was from a working-class background. Consciously or not, those who made the hiring decision (middle-class academics and administrators) did not feel quite comfortable with this person, but framed the decision by deciding that this candidate didn't seem likely to fit in at the institution in question. I believe this type of decision occurs more often than we would like to think.

These issues of privilege, and particularly those of social class, need to be further explored in our professional venues. One way to do so is through academics' sharing their experiences, their stories. In the next section, I discuss reasons for my belief that personal narrative can be a powerful and effective form of scholarly writing, and my reasons for choosing to incorporate personal narrative into my writing, as I have done in this book.

Personal Narrative in Academic Writing

This book is not written in a typical academic style; rather, it is written in a hybrid genre; it presents personal narratives in the context of more traditional academic writing. The personal stories are drawn from my own life and the lives of those I interact with, especially my students and my professional colleagues. All of the stories, even the childhood and outside-of-work stories, connect with my life as an educator and scholar. The more traditional academic writing builds on my interests in, and prior research and publications on, issues in the interrelated fields of TESOL, Applied Linguistics, Second Language Education, Language and Literacy Education, Literary Studies, and Gender and Sexualities Studies. The memoirist Patricia Hampl (1999) alludes to this connection between our experiences and the issues we care about when she says, "Instinctively, we go to our store of private associations for our authority to speak of these weighty issues" (p. 31). She further describes memoir as "the intersection of narration and reflection, of storytelling and essay writing. It can present its story *and* consider the meaning of the story" (p. 33). This is what I am aiming for in my own mixture of story, context, interpretation, and application. My hope is that the various types of writing that are combined and intertwined here, and the various types of writing in the professional and other literature drawn on in this book, inform each other, and that the combinations illuminate important professional and social/political questions that educators struggle with.

A very basic reason for the introduction of narrative into academic writing may have to do with the universal human need and desire for story, something Coles (1989) terms "the call of stories." Doris Lessing, in her 2007 Nobel Prize for Literature acceptance speech, reminds us that "The storyteller is deep inside everyone of us. The story-maker is always with us . . . for it is our imaginations which shape us, keep us, create us—for good and for ill" (Lessing, 2007). There is also a human urge to tell one's *own* story, thus the recent predominance of personal blogs, and of autobiographies and memoirs on the bestseller lists and, now, in academe.

In recent years, there has been an increased flexibility about which kinds of writing constitute acceptable scholarly writing; qualitative and ethnographic research and narrative inquiry have become somewhat more common and accepted. There is an enhanced understanding that there is nothing sacred about quantitative research, that no research or writing is truly objective, and that various types of research and writing can and do add different and valuable perspectives to the bodies of knowledge and scholarship in most disciplines (Bateson, 1994; Bruner, 1991; Geertz, 1995; Polkinghorne, 1988). Czarniawska (2004), for example, writes of the "narrative turn" in social sciences. Some publications about qualitative research and academic writing specifically address questions of narrative research; examples include Burdell and Swadener (1999); Clandinin and Connelly (2000); Daiute and Lightfoot (2004); and Witherell and Noddings (1991). Such "narrative inquiry" in academic research and writing can provide a new and useful way of illuminating research questions and issues, and of making academic writing more accessible as well. As Christine Pearson Casanave and I put it in an earlier publication (Casanave & Vandrick, 2003a),

> narratives allow for understanding and connection
> in ways that straight exposition does not. Truth
> in academic writing, particularly in the more sci-
> entific fields, has been characterized as objective,
> as written in the third person, as distanced from
> personal feelings and experiences. Language educa-
> tion, especially ESL, was grounded in applied linguis-
> tics, which considered and perhaps still considers
> itself a science, so these attitudes have been the
> foundation of scholarly writing in many language-

> related fields. Yet we contend, as do an increasing
> number of scholars in our field as well as related
> fields, that there is another kind of truth to be
> obtained from narratives, stories, and first-person
> viewpoints, which people use to construct their
> realities and interpret their experiences. (p. 2)

As a feminist scholar, another reason that I am drawn to narrative as scholarly inquiry is that many feminist scholars consider such narratives to have "epistemological and methodological value because it is through narrative that personal experience—a rich source of knowledge—can be shared and theorized" (Sharkey, 2004, p. 498). One of the earliest and most inspiring of scholars to write about the importance of story for women was Carolyn Heilbrun, especially in her groundbreaking 1988 book, *Writing a Woman's Life*; it is a book I treasured when it was first published, and treasure still. Gender issues, and feminist analysis, are an integral part of my own life, stories, scholarship, and teaching.

The use of personal or autobiographical narrative in academic writing is still even less common than other types of narrative, such as ethnographic accounts. However, personal narrative has been more frequently discussed, employed, and published in recent years in various academic disciplines. In the move to more qualitative inquiry in many academic disciplines, some have argued the value of autoethnography, in which "the researcher is the subject of the text," and "researchers conduct and write ethnographies of their own experiences" (Denzin & Lincoln, 2002, p. xii). Willard-Traub (2006) points out that "Increasingly . . . approaches to writing that incorporate autobiography and personal narrative are being used by scholars not simply as means for meditating on lived experience, but also as methods of scholarly analysis and argumentation" (p. 424). She adds that the "turn toward reflective writing across the disciplines attests to the influence of cultural studies, feminist studies, and epistemologies that insist on the local and the 'everyday' not only as valid objects of inquiry, but also as valid sources of authority" (p. 425).

Some of the prominent scholars in various fields who have felt constrained by the limitations of traditional academic writing and have chosen to experiment with employing personal narrative in their academic work include anthropologist Ruth Behar (1993), sociologist Carolyn Ellis (1997), French Studies scholar Alice Kaplan (1993), English literature scholar Shirley Geok-lin Lim (1996), sociologist Laurel Richardson (1997), and law scholar Patricia Williams (1991); collections of such writing across the disciplines include Freedman and Frey (2003). Examples in the field of education but focusing on certain populations of academics are Dews and Law's (1995) collection of essays by academics from working class backgrounds, Freeman and Schmidt's (2000) collected stories of women teachers, and Li and Beckett's (2006) edited volume on and by Asian women academics.

In English and composition studies, there have been several "special issues" of journals on personal narrative (e.g., Gebhardt, 1992; Hindman, 2001, 2003), and numerous scholars have used personal narrative in their published academic writing (e.g., Bishop, 1997; Bloom, 1992; Haroian-Guerin, 1999; Herron, 1992; McCracken & Larson, 1998; Roen, Brown, & Enos, 1999; Schmidt, 1998; Trimmer, 1997). The increasing popularity of personal narrative in these fields may be partly due to the very nature and emphasis of the disciplines: a focus on writing.

Teacher educators have also used stories to enable prospective teachers to better understand "the richness of experience and practice, . . . the struggles and triumphs of teaching, . . . the life of classrooms" (Phillion, 2005, p. 1). Connelly and Clandinin, in particular, have been leaders in valuing "teacher knowledge," stating that "stories, . . . narratives of experience, are both personal—reflecting a person's life history—and social—reflecting the milieu, the contexts in which teachers live" (1999, p. 2).

TESOL scholars have been much slower to write about personal experiences in academe, but since the mid-1990s, there have been several examples of such writing, including the following edited collections: Belcher and Connor's collection of stories of multiliterate scholars

(2001); Blanton and Kroll's collection of reflections by seasoned scholars and teachers in TESOL composition (2002); Braine's volume of autobiographical writing of nonnative teachers of English (1999); Casanave and Schecter's set of personal narratives by teachers about how they became teachers (1997); Casanave and Vandrick's contributors' essays on their varied experiences as scholarly writers (2003b); and the stories of racial minority educators in TESOL (Curtis & Romney, 2006). Individual articles or books employing personal narrative include Casanave and Sosa (2007); Kouritzin (2004); Lin et al. (2004); Sharkey (2004); Vandrick (2001a); and Woo (1999). Other scholars who include some personal narrative, and whose strongly personal authorial voices are integral parts of their books, include Clarke (2003, 2007). TESOL scholars who have written *about* narrative as research include Bell (2002); Johnson and Golombek (2002); and Pavlenko (2001, 2002, 2007).

These scholars and their work have paved the way for others, including myself, to experiment with new forms of academic writing. In this book, as stated at the beginning of this section, I employ a hybrid genre, focusing on personal or autobiographical narrative, but always in the context of theory and the professional literature about the topics I address through my narrative. Most of my narratives focus on my own experiences as an educator and scholar, both inside and out of the classroom and university, as well as on the experiences of some of my students and my fellow educators. In order to provide theoretical/academic context for these stories, in each chapter I draw on related scholarly literature about the areas on which I focus. As Bell (2002) points out, narrative inquiry "requires going beyond the use of narrative as rhetorical structure, that is, simply telling stories, to an analytic examination of the underlying insights and assumptions that the story illustrates" (p. 208); this blending of story and analysis is my goal in this book. Nash (2004) calls this type of combining of genres "scholarly personal narrative" (p. 4), and states that such writing differs from memoir and autobiography because the personal narrative is organized "around themes, issues, constructs, and concepts that carry larger, more universalizable meanings for readers" (p. 30). Spigelman (2004) asserts that "Personal writing can do serious academic work; it can make rational arguments; it can merge appropriately with academic discourse" (p. 2), and goes on to employ the terms "personal academic discourse" (p. 3) and, her preferred term, "personal academic argument" (p. 10), to describe this "blended genre" (p. 2).

Reflecting and writing on one's own experiences is not easy. It is difficult to gain the necessary perspective to be insightful about one's own life and experiences. Even when we achieve insights, it is often difficult to articulate them in ways that are accessible to readers. Telling our stories draws on different skills than our usual academic writing does. And although we now understand that all knowledge, all research, all "truth" is subjective, when we tell our own stories we must acknowledge that such telling involves fallible memories, as well as more interpretation, more subjectivity, than most other types of research and writing. Further, it is somewhat anxiety-producing, even frightening, to look deeply into ourselves, and to expose aspects of ourselves and our experiences to our readers, many of whom may be our professional peers as well; if writers are truly being honest in telling their stories, they make themselves vulnerable in a rather public way.

In addition, we must acknowledge that in telling our own stories, we are always telling stories of those around us as well, and we have an obligation to them not to violate their privacy or to misrepresent them. We can protect their confidentiality, where it is appropriate, by providing pseudonyms and omitting identifying details. The question of representation of others is a more difficult one. Are we representing others accurately? Fairly? Are we careful not to violate their privacy, their dignity? Do we recognize ways in which our own cultural and other identities and positionalities may affect how we perceive and portray others? Do we claim to speak for others, those with identities different than our own, in a way that would not be acceptable to people with those identities? These are all difficult questions that must be kept in mind when portraying others and their stories. (See Tierney & Lincoln, 1997, for further exploration of these topics.) In this book, I will address some of these issues in more detail as I describe my own struggles with them.

Despite the increasing acceptance of personal writing, autobiographical or personal writing is still questioned or even denigrated by many in academe, and this denigration may have negative consequences for a scholar's career and reputation. Some scholars who have used alternative writing styles and topics have spoken of feeling marginalized when doing so (Dean, 1998; Richardson, 1997). Some young scholars have been cautioned not to do personal writing early in their careers, or at least to balance such writing with other more traditional academic writing. It is true that most of the pioneers of personal writing in academe have been well-established scholars whose solid reputations could withstand negative perceptions of their experimentation with alternative, more personal topics and types of writing. For example, in the (overlapping) fields of composition and English, some of the early writers of personal essays published in academic journals were Nancy K. Miller (1991, 1997, 2002), Nancy Sommers (1992, 1993, 1998), and Jane Tompkins (1987, 1990, 1996), all well-known scholars with secure positions in academe.

In this book, another way in which I deviate from traditional academic writing is that, although I am not writing specifically about literature, I also sometimes draw on literary sources, especially fiction. I have loved reading, especially reading fiction, ever since I was a child; I have undergraduate and graduate degrees in English literature; I have taught literature, written about literature, especially about teaching literature (Vandrick, 1993, 1994b, 1996, 1997a, 1997c, 2003); and I continue to read dozens of novels, short story collections, and memoirs every year. I believe that literature represents the deepest wisdom of each culture, and I further believe that literature can provide insights that illuminate almost any topic.

I hope that the stories in this book, while not claiming to be representative of the experiences of all educators, will shed light on some aspects of the lives and experiences of educators and their students, especially (but definitely not only) in the (closely related) fields of second language education, applied linguistics, and TESOL. Further, I hope that these narratives, in conjunction with the more traditional academic exposition in which they are set, will stimulate thought and discussion about the role of privilege in education.

Overview of the Book's Structure

This book consists of ten chapters. All of the chapters address issues of privilege as manifested in the lives and work of educators, especially second language educators, and most especially ESOL educators. A foundational assumption throughout the book is that teachers and students do not come to their classrooms and work as blank slates, but bring all their identities and experiences, whether they show or discuss them openly or not. Each chapter includes, in some way and to some degree, attention to educators' and scholars' personal lives, teaching lives, and writing lives, in other words, to educators and scholars as "whole persons"; some chapters focus on one of the three aspects (personal, teaching, and writing) more than others. Many chapters also address issues of privilege as they can be seen in students' personal lives and classroom experiences. In all cases, much attention is given to intersections of various types: between students and teachers, between teaching and scholarship, between institutions and their participants, among each person's multiple identities, and among the various identities of various participants in the educational world. Some of the experiences and examples I describe refer specifically to ESOL settings, some do not, but in all cases they address aspects of the multifaceted lives of ESOL (and other) teachers and scholars.

After this introductory chapter that you are reading now, the book continues with Chapter 2, "ESL and the Colonial Legacy: A Teacher Faces Her 'Missionary Kid' Past." This chapter employs personal narrative as well as perspectives gained from post-colonial studies as a lens to analyze connections between, on the one hand, my experiences as a child of Christian missionaries in India and, on the other hand, my years of teaching ESOL. I discuss implications for the field of TESOL. Chapter 3, "Tea and TESOL," attempts to demonstrate how certain physical objects and their related associations and ceremonies reflect one's experiences, thoughts, and aspirations, and are symbolic of certain types of privilege. For me, tea (the word, the physical material, the meal, the connotations) symbolizes comfort, my childhood in barely post-colonial India, my Anglophilia, my beloved English novels, women's groups, and the nourishing of community, among other associations; it is also a source of ambivalence because of its postcolonial and social class associations. I make connections between these various associations and my life and work in international education.

In Chapter 4, "Shifting Sites, Shifting Identities: A 30-Year Perspective," I examine the effects of institutional contexts on the careers and lives of ESOL educators and students. As an example, I describe the institution where I have taught over a period of more than thirty years as a site of some of the historical and material factors that influence and shape the field of ESOL and its participants. This chapter includes attention to some of the specific "on the ground" issues that educators deal with in interacting with their institutions and working conditions. I examine the power of institutions through the perspective of privilege. Chapter 5, "Fathers and Mentors," is a tribute to my own father and to the academic "fathers" who have mentored, helped, and supported me in my career; it also examines the aspects of privilege that allow such support. In Chapter 6, I turn to the topic of "Gender, Class, and the Balanced Life." Although there are many aspects of gender and class that could be discussed, some of which I have addressed in other publications, here I focus on a critical, even urgent, topic for many academic women: how women in education—both students and faculty—struggle with balancing work and family in a society that often makes this balancing act very difficult. After framing the issue, I illustrate the dilemma with the story of a female graduate student whom I observed and interviewed over some time, and the ways in which her gender and her social class impacted her experiences as she attempted to balance preparing for a career with having a family. Chapter 7, "Sexual Identity and Education," continues to examine the impact of social class on international and immigrant students and instructors, this time at the intersection of class and sexual orientation. I know that many educators struggle, as I did and do, with whether and how to address sexual identity issues in their classrooms and institutions. I argue that we educators, no matter what our own sexual identities are, must acknowledge the presence of students and faculty of various sexual identities, and must grapple with how to support and educate all our students and colleagues, in order to ensure equity for all. I explore these issues partly through describing my own personal journey to better understanding of, and to speaking and writing in professional venues about, LGBT issues; I hope that my experiences will be of use to other educators.

In the next two chapters, I shift my focus toward the topic of scholarly writing, and how educators can incorporate their research and writing into their personal and academic lives. I also discuss the issues of privilege that allow some but not others to engage in research and writing. In the first of these two chapters about writing, Chapter 8, I write about my own path toward scholarly writing; as a late-blooming writer, I title this chapter "On Beginning to Write at 40." This chapter explores obstacles—personal, social, and institutional—that academics, especially women academics, may need to overcome in order to become published scholars. The second chapter about writing, Chapter 9, celebrates "The Power of Writing Groups." It includes examples from my own several writing groups and related groups, all of which in various ways provide vital support, assistance, and encouragement to my academic and writing life; I then examine the types of privilege necessary in order to obtain such support.

The book concludes with Chapter 10, "The Aging Educator," in which I reflect on my more than 35 years of teaching and on what I have learned, in the contexts of how the world has changed, and how the fields of applied linguistics and TESOL have changed, during that time period. I discuss the advantages and disadvantages of being an aging educator, especially a female aging educator, and again, examine intersections among age and other identities.

Questions for further reflection and discussion are included at the end of the volume (see pages 157–162).

Throughout this book, I hope to convey my belief that entering and sustaining a teaching life involves recognition that we are whole, multifaceted persons, leading complex lives, in multiple contexts; the same is true for our students. Our teaching and scholarly work cannot and should not be isolated or separated from our backgrounds, our various identities, our living conditions, or our beliefs, nor from those of our students and colleagues. The topics addressed in this book are elements that form strands of the web of our connections with each other. That is not to say that any or all of these factors will necessarily be focuses of our classroom teaching or our scholarly writing, but that it is critical to recognize and reflect on the contexts they provide and the ways in which they influence our work.

With this discussion of privilege, and of the role of personal narrative in academic writing, as foundation and context for the rest of the book, I invite you, the reader, to proceed to the following chapters, to peruse my stories, and to make connections with your own stories. I welcome your responses, and would be honored to hear your stories as well.

Chapter 2

ESL and the Colonial Legacy: A Teacher Faces Her "Missionary Kid" Past[1]

Note to the Reader:

As this essay was originally published in 1999, I would like to share with readers the reasons that it was important to me to begin (after the introduction) the book in your hands with this chapter. First, it is chronologically the foundation for the other chapters, as it makes connections between my childhood and my adult career as an educator. Second, it was one of my earliest publications focusing on the theme of this book: privilege and its consequences. Third, it was my first academic publication that included personal narrative. When I wrote and published it, I was quite nervous about the personal aspect. It felt

---

[1] This essay is a very slightly revised version of one that was originally published as Vandrick, S. (1999). ESL and the colonial legacy: A teacher faces her "missionary kid" past. In G. Haroian-Guerin (Ed.), *The personal narrative: Writing ourselves as teachers and scholars* (pp. 63–74). Portland, ME: Calendar Islands Publishers.

a bit frightening to write these candid stories in which I was not always portrayed in a positive light; I wondered if the piece was too personal, too revealing. I also wondered if reading it would hurt my parents' feelings; fortunately, they were very open to my reflections and interpretations, and as supportive of my writing as they have always been. At the same time that I experienced these various types of trepidation, I was exhilarated by the process of writing the piece, because it led me to at least partly understand the connections between my childhood experiences as a "missionary kid" and my adult experiences teaching ESOL in a way that I would probably not have done without the long, tangled thinking and writing process that resulted in this piece. I also wondered if publishing this very personal piece would be judged to be unscholarly, or worse, self-indulgent. And some readers may indeed have perceived the piece in that way. But it also received positive atten-tion, both when it was originally published and when it was later anthologized. It was partly the self-discovery and satisfaction I experienced in writing this piece, and partly the positive reception it received from many colleagues and students, that encouraged me to continue pursuing this type of personal writing as part of my scholarly work, and eventually led me to write this book.

A hidden aspect of teaching ESL students is the colonial legacy of the profession, a legacy that in some senses taints those of us who teach these students. This legacy can involve, on some unspoken and mainly unacknowledged level, a feeling of superiority of West to East, of English to other (especially non-European) languages, so that teaching English becomes a kind of preaching "a better way" to the "natives." We who teach ESL classes, as well as composition classes that include non-native English speakers, must confront the possible consequences of this colonial shadow.

This "colonial" attitude is not (generally) intentional. And of course what we ESL teachers do is "good," isn't it? Isn't learning new languages intrinsically a good thing? And isn't English an important and even essential (perhaps the most important and most essential) worldwide language? These have been basic assumptions in the field of ESL. And, after all, don't students *demand* English classes?

All of the above assumptions may be legitimate. But we ESL teachers must at least think about the possibility of a "colonial shadow" over our profession, along with the effects of such a shadow. Do we on some level believe English is superior? And therefore that English speakers are superior? And that native speakers—and especially speakers of Western Englishes—are particularly superior? And do we believe that those who learn it gain some of our superiority (only some—they can never quite catch up)? If we do in fact believe these things on some level, all of these beliefs enhance our self-image as ESL teachers; look how "good" we are, sharing the valuable treasure of our language, and by extension, our culture and our power.

I believe that all of us who teach English language and writing classes to nonnative speakers of English are affected by this colonial legacy, but some of us have been even more immersed in it than others because of our life circumstances. We don't often look at our own backgrounds and how they lead us to teach ESL, and how they affect the way we teach. We are more likely to discuss *students'* backgrounds—nationality, ethnicity, race, class, gender, educational background, and so on—and how these factors affect their motivation, achievement, and classroom interactions. But it makes sense that instructors' backgrounds would have an enormous effect on their motivation, teaching philosophies and styles, and attitudes toward and interactions with students. Elsewhere (Vandrick, 1997e) I have explored the effects of both students' and teachers' identities, particularly hidden identities, on classroom interactions. Similarly, Spack (1997) points out that

> As teachers and researchers, we have been reading our classrooms—including actual texts and students as texts—but, for the most part, we have not turned our gaze on ourselves. Yet given the

> cultural work that many of us are doing, we need
> to understand who we are as historical, political,
> social, and cultural beings in order to gain a fuller
> sense of the complexity of the relationship between
> teacher, student, and text. (p. 10)

It is becoming increasingly recognized that one of the best ways to build knowledge is to share stories (see, for example, Casanave & Schecter, 1997; Coles, 1989). Some of those who have reminded us of this are black storytellers, oral historians, and feminists in consciousness-raising groups. In particular, autobiography can be powerful. Hesford (1997) writes that because "teachers reward students for writing texts that preserve myths of objectivity and the impartiality of scholarship," for students to write autobiographical texts in academic settings can be powerful because of its allowing of room to write "against the grain by challenging and displacing the academy's authority through constructing disruptive subject positions and discourse" (p. 134). Although faculty/scholars are expected to write in such a way that will "preserve the myths of objectivity and the impartiality of scholarship," writing autobiographically may provide another way for them as well to make knowledge.

We are beginning to see more "teachers' stories." Particular aspects of a teacher's family or individual history may affect her or his teaching. Clearly each teacher has her or his own story, and we cannot generalize about ESL (or any) teachers based on any one story, but perhaps if we share enough stories, we will begin to see patterns.

In India

Thus I share here my own story of having been an "MK," a "missionary kid," the child of missionary parents. I have only recently looked at this story in a new light, a light made possible by more than thirty years of distance. I grew up as an "MK" in India, graciously dispensing gifts, hand-me-downs, prizes, trinkets, wisdom, religion, and Western culture to the "natives." My parents—and by extension my brothers and I— were caught up, unwittingly, in a historical phenomenon: the colonial spread of Western culture to the East, whether through government, trade, or religion. And on the part of some, at least, this phenomenon was well intentioned. Doris Lessing, whose British father worked in both Persia (now Iran) and Rhodesia (now Zimbabwe), writes of her parents' belief that "they represented God's will, working by agency of the British Empire, for the good of the world" (qtd. in Schinto, 1997, p. 31). In retrospect, I can see how immersed we were in a very colonial mode.

Now I teach ESL to students of the world, graciously dispensing the gifts, prizes, and wisdom made available through the English language, "American culture," and academic skills for the American university. What is the connection? I used to believe that I became an ESL teacher partly because of my growing up overseas, which gave me a simple interest in other cultures and other languages. Now, many years after leaving India, and eventually beginning to teach ESL, I am finally beginning to see and acknowledge another, more complicated aspect of the connection. Was it being steeped in the colonial project—albeit indirectly, through a Canadian church mission—that made ESL teaching seem oh-so-familiar and oh-so-comfortable that very first day I, as an eager and naïve graduate assistant, stood up in front of my first ESL class full of "natives" from Asia, Africa, and the Middle East? Was I once again in the position of the generous but condescending Lady Bountiful dispensing my valued linguistic and cultural favors to the uncivilized (non-Western) natives?

When, years after growing up in India as an "MK," I "fell into" ESL teaching without consciously planning to, I immediately felt "at home." The obvious explanation for my immediate sense of comfort with ESL teaching might be that I was used to being in a different culture and to hearing and speaking several languages, that I enjoyed interaction with people from different cultures, and that those factors in combination with my love of language and literature made ESL teaching a logical and happy "fit" for me. For years I assumed that this innocuous explanation was true. And in a way, it was and is in fact true. But looked at from a different angle, and from the vantage point of nearly three decades of teaching and thinking, there is another truth, a perhaps less straightforward and comfortable truth. I was a child in a missionary family; my parents went to India to provide assistance to Indian people. Let me say here that my parents are the kindest, most well-intentioned people one could meet, and that they dedicated a good part of their life, at considerable sacrifice, to give their talents and skills to help people. My father was a doctor who did surgery in village hospitals, set up clinics in the jungle, and worked with lepers. My mother helped in hospitals and schools, while raising four children. They made an enormous and tangible contribution, changing and even saving many people's lives. They did so because of their religious faith, but they did not impose their religion on anyone. (I realize that the latter is not true of all missionaries, but it was true of my parents.) I myself could never and will never make the kind of sacrifices most missionaries had to make, and it is unlikely that anything I do will change people's lives and help people in such concrete ways as my parents' work did.

But—despite these caveats—there was a "missionary mentality" that I unconsciously absorbed. My brothers and I grew up in the India of the 1950s and 1960s, just after Indian Independence. We were very attached to India, as most children are attached to the places where they grow up. My life there is a huge and essential part of who I am. But in many senses we were never really part of India. Since we moved there so soon after the British had left India, the colonial tradition was still very strong, still very much present. And my parents and their North American colleagues had clearly come from the West to share their (by implication superior) Western religion, expertise, and resources. Although India had so recently become independent, Indians still deferred (at least outwardly) to whites, still the "sahibs," in many ways. It takes a long time for cultural change to catch up with political change.

Although my family was far from wealthy by North American standards, our house was much larger than the other houses in the village we lived in, and we had several servants to manage the cooking, housework, and garden, all of which demanded much time and energy, as there were very few labor-saving appliances available in India at that time. We took the servants for granted, and were genuinely fond of some of them, but there was not a sense of equality with them.

The closest relationships we children had with Indians were with our ayahs (Indian nannies) when we were little, especially one named Perongani, whom we missed terribly when she left to get married. Although my mother didn't work full-time when we were small, we spent a lot of time with this young Indian woman and were very fond of her. We thought she was beautiful. We were sometimes naughty and disobedient, and we somehow knew she didn't have any ultimate authority over us. But we loved her and felt a great sense of loss when she left. When another, less pretty, less "fun" ayah took her place, we were unhappy and uncooperative. Our story echoes those of the British and other colonial families in India, Africa, the Philippines, and elsewhere with ayahs and servants. Our story also resonates with those of white families in the American South with black "mammies," and with those of American families with Mexican nannies/house-keepers even now. In all of these stories, there was between the families and ayahs/mammies/nannies a strange closeness, intimate yet decidedly unequal, unbalanced.

We children played with Indian children, but not much, and again, not on a truly equal basis. I remember with embarrassment that we used to show off our North American toys, enjoying the attention from the Indian children who crowded around to see them.

Arriving back in India after three years home in the United States and Canada on furlough, we four children greeted our newly delivered big boxes of belongings

with fervor and raced to unpack them and try them out. We took everything out on the wide veranda that circled our spacious bungalow, on a compound set back from the village road and surrounded by gardens and trees. We ostentatiously set out our pile of bicycles, sports equipment, toys . . . all the accouterments of Western childhood, commonplace "back home" but envied treasures here in an Indian village. We then proceeded to play with them all, systematically yet somewhat frantically. I particularly remember jumping on a pogo stick over and over . . . bounce, bounce, bounce. . . . We were still unsettled, a little hyperactive, and were acting out a bit, showing off. My brothers played an impromptu game of badminton. We threw Frisbees wildly, and laughed loudly. We knew quite well that we had an audience, that we were objects of curiosity, and we assumed that we were objects of admiration and envy. We were very aware that crowds of village children were watching us from the road, through the fence around the compound, and though we didn't speak of it to each other, we each knew that the others knew that we were performing. We were reaching out to connect with the Indian children, but in a way that was in effect establishing our "superior" place in the hierarchy. Bounce, bounce . . . sneak a look at the crowds of children watching . . . affect nonchalance . . . bounce, bounce, bounce some more. . . .

Our mission ran a boarding school for Indian village girls that was next door to our compound. I rarely played with "the boarding girls." Sometimes I would swing on the rope swing hanging from a tree next to the wall around the boarding school, and as I sailed into the sky, I would sing, partly for the benefit of the Indian girls. I imagined them envying me my swing, my big house, my freedom, and my obviously superior position in the world. One of the few times I visited the boarding school and spent time with the girls, it was viewed on both sides as a kind of royal visit. I was about ten years old. I was treated with great deference (though I have no idea what they were actually thinking about me or about their being required to appear deferential to me). It seemed quite justified to me that they should be happy I was visiting them. I brought some candy and small gifts. In any case, the girls gathered around me, politely praising me and asking me questions. They were particularly interested in my hair since it was light brown, *almost blond. They asked if they could comb it, and they did. A day or two after this visit, I found I had head lice. I felt, mostly unconsciously, that it was shameful to have lice, and that this shameful condition was a natural consequence of mixing too much with the boarding school girls. The proper order of things had been upset, the proper separation between "them" and "us" had been violated. I never played with the boarding girls again.*

When we went to the local church and sat through long services in a language we did not know, or when we went to the Christmas party at the hospital or at one of the schools, it was because it was our duty to do so, to "make an appearance" there; in fact, there was a sense of noblesse oblige. *The missionary family feeling of* noblesse oblige *became, perhaps, most explicit in the Christmas parties we gave, first for our servants and then for the workers in the small mission hospital my father ran. A large meal was served. Everyone sat on the floor on the veranda, and steaming food was piled onto the stitched-together banana leaves that served as plates. Curiously, I cannot remember who cooked and served the meals for the servants. Did they double as cooks/servants and guests? Did my parents hire other servants to serve our servants? After the meal, gifts were handed out to each person. One of the adults would call the name of each servant or worker, and indicate the gift intended for that person (most often a piece of clothing, or a length of material to be used for clothing). We children were invited to hand the gifts out as each person stepped forward. We looked forward to this ritual, which allowed us to feel both generous and superior. How did the adult Indians feel, having to act subservient and grateful to white children handing them gifts?*

For a large part of the year, we four children were away at a boarding school in a hill resort town with other children of Western missionaries, diplomats, and businessmen. Although we were thousands of miles from "home," we easily preserved the rituals of American adolescence, only a year or two behind the latest trends "back home." We saw Hollywood movies, listened to and danced to American and British rock music, and envied those who had recently been in the United States and had brought back the latest music and clothes and slang. It was assumed that our time in India was temporary, and that we would all go home eventually; as much as we loved India, our futures would not be there. I have a very clear memory of thinking, one day when I was about six or seven years old, that of course the United States and Canada were the "main" places, in other words the center of the universe, and that everywhere else was peripheral. Later on, after graduation from high school, when one of my fellow students, another "missionary kid," chose to stay in India for the rest of his life, most of us felt he had "gone native," and couldn't imagine doing the same.

I do not mean to say that we—the "we" of my family, and the "we" of many of the Western people who lived in India—didn't respect or value Indians; we did. But in day-to-day life, we had our own way of doing things, our own lives, and it seemed quite natural to us that these did not intersect very much with the lives of the people who lived there, the Indians. We didn't question the situation; it was just the way things were. There was an implicit assumption of the superiority of Western people and ways, although we would have been surprised and embarrassed to hear that assumption spoken aloud. If questioned, we would probably have denied that we had such an assumption, but we would have done so with a vague sense of uneasiness.

Becoming an ESL Teacher

When I began graduate school, my assistantship involved teaching ESL to international university students, and from the first day of class I loved the teaching and felt "at home" in the ESL classroom. I assumed that I felt so comfortable and happy in the teaching situation at least partly because it reminded me of my childhood years overseas, and that I was a world citizen type after all, despite my six years away from that identification. But now I wonder if that immediate connection was, at least partly, with the colonial aspects of my missionary kid background, rather than with my living in India *per se*. Perhaps the teaching situation "clicked" for me because (unconsciously) it was a kind of "ministering to the natives" all over again. They—in this case the international students in my classes—lacked something that I had (the English language, knowledge of Western academe and culture), something that I could magnanimously provide for them. I could be the generous colonial lady, or perhaps the missionary coming to "help" the natives. Also, perhaps, this situation provided a gratifying ego boost; when one teaches, one is in a position of knowledge and power, and teaching one's native language, one is clearly "in the right" and can't be easily challenged. Again, all of this was unconscious. . . .

"Thank you, teacher," my students often said, smiling at and sometimes even bowing to me. They seemed so grateful, so appreciative. How kind I felt, how wise, how generous.

I also strongly believed that I was free of prejudice because I had grown up in India, experiencing living with people of various ethnic backgrounds and economic levels. But I have recently become much more conscious of some of the sense of privilege I carry, along with some of the unconscious racism that infects almost everyone with privilege, including "colonial" privilege. Reading McIntosh (1988) and then Wildman (1996) on "white privilege" has helped me understand how this unconscious, absolutely taken for granted, privilege pervades every aspect of a white person's life.

I have also realized that when students are not "properly appreciative," I feel, unconsciously or consciously, somewhat annoyed, even resentful. I find myself feeling, to my surprise, that they *should* appreciate this wonderful opportunity they have to study English in the United States. And they shouldn't criticize too much: not me, nor English, nor the United States. . . . Sometimes students come uncannily close to home with their comments, little realizing how I may react. . . .

Recently my advanced ESL reading class read Chinua Achebe's (1953/1994) short story "Dead Man's Path," which describes an African headmaster who has received his education in missionary schools. He prides himself on his education and his modern attitude, and condescendingly scoffs at the beliefs of the villagers regarding the spirits of their ancestors. During the class discussion, I spoke about colonialism, including the missionaries' role in it, and expounded upon the difficulties caused when colonial cultures clashed with traditional cultures. One of my students interrupted, "So, missionary means arrogant?" "No, no," I replied. "Well, SOMETIMES some missionaries are arrogant, but not all." ("Not my parents," I think.) How can I explain the problems of colonialism, yet not criticize all colonizers, all missionaries? I feel myself becoming defensive. Should I tell my class that my parents were missionaries, that I grew up as a missionary kid? No, it would be too complicated to explain. I don't want to deal with explaining. . . . So, perhaps wisely, or perhaps out of cowardice, I don't reveal my personal connection to the question, and we move on to analyze other aspects of the story.

English, the Colonial Legacy, and Privilege

This sense of privilege, along with its part in the colonial legacy influencing those teaching the English language, has been discussed by some theorists and researchers in ESL and linguistics, particularly those concerned with language planning (see, e.g., Canagarajah, 1993; Phillipson, 1992; Tollefson, 1991, 1995). Areas in which the quasi-colonial attitude is questioned include arguments that immigrants in the United States are taught a kind of utilitarian "survival" English, an English that will be "good enough" for their needs and that will help them to fit in to their (fairly lowly) place in the system. Auerbach and Burgess (1985), for example, are concerned that "Survival ESL" curricula "prepare students for subservient social roles and reinforce hierarchical relations within the classroom" (p. 475). Tollefson "challenges the survival English taught to refugees . . . for its ideological content (e.g., refugees are taught that if they work hard and apply themselves, they too will be equipped to join our consumer society)" (paraphrased in Leki, 1997, p. 241). We especially note the possible signs of the colonial legacy as we see the English language being taught and proliferating in non-Western countries. In many countries, English is being promoted as the language of technology and commerce, the language that is necessary to compete in the world today. In non-Western countries that already have a history of using the English language, those colonized by England or the United States, we can see a different aspect of the colonial attitude: British or American English is held up as the standard, and the various other Englishes that have developed, such as Indian English, are considered inferior and even laughable by many. In recent years we have been sensitized to this type of condescension by such authorities on World Englishes as Kachru (1993).

Here, however, although my thinking draws on all of the above sources, I particularly want to explore the way we as individual teachers—"we" signifying, broadly, ESL instructors who are native speakers of Western Englishes—may be unconsciously influenced by the colonial mode of thinking and how it may manifest itself in our teaching. The word *unconsciously* is critical, because most ESL teachers are well-intentioned and caring people. The colonial aspect I discuss here is something that operates below the surface, something that we have absorbed with our culture in many subtle ways.

Even in classrooms that are not specifically ESL, but are, for example, freshman writing classes with students from various national, ethnic, and cultural backgrounds (the kind of classroom that is increasingly common in today's institutions of higher education), there is an imposition of Western values and of standard English. De and Gregory (1997) state that in such classrooms, "Students whose thinking differs substantially from or lies on the margins of the epistemic practices dominant in a

Western metropolitan academy are liable to be 'colonized' by the theoretical methods they encounter on entering" (p. 118). They go on to say that "Writing teachers widely recognize that culturally diverse students who succeed in the United States university do so because they have been successfully socialized into Western argumentative discourse. This socialization often occurs at the expense of students' culture-specific ways of interacting with reality" (p. 119). For students in such writing classes as well as those in ESL classes, there is a need to learn Western academic discourse, yet a need to preserve their own styles of writing, which are determined by their own cultural assumptions and practices. The conflict between these two needs can be very painful (Fox, 1994; Shen, 1989).

Colonial Images, Colonial Attitudes

I have gone on to teach for many years, and have continued to enjoy it and feel it is a way to make a contribution. But the realizations outlined here have made me question much about that teaching. If in fact I (and perhaps other ESL teachers) am influenced by the colonial legacy, in what ways is that manifested in the classroom? Shafiei (1997) quotes an adult ESL student describing his teacher's behavior as follows: "My teachers were kind, but I was ashamed to talk because I felt like a little baby, and my teacher acted like my mother" (p. 10). Shafiei notes that many ESL instructors speak loudly and make large gestures, and goes on to point out that ESL students often feel condescended to, including being excessively and exaggeratedly praised for any achievements, as if teachers are surprised by the ESL students' success. Also, do ESL teachers, along with much of American academe, always use the West, and particularly the United States, as the central reference point, so that everything else is marginalized, and dealt with only in terms of its relationship to the West, or in terms of how it measures up to Western standards? Is the English language, and particularly the "standard" English of the United States or Great Britain, central, with all other languages, especially non-European languages, marginal? Do we feel that we are giving our students a gift by sharing our language and culture with them, and that they should be properly grateful for this gracious gift, and should show their gratitude appropriately? Do we, consciously or unconsciously, penalize students who don't appear to be properly cognizant of the favor we are doing them, and therefore don't show proper signs of gratitude?

It is not fair to generalize about other ESL faculty from my story or my speculations here. However, I believe that my story may to some extent reflect the experiences and attitudes of other American or British ESL teachers who are children of missionaries, and perhaps of other ESL teachers who grew up in countries where (Western) Englishes were not the first language. It is possible that my story also overlaps in some ways the experiences of those who have themselves worked in countries outside the United States and Great Britain (and Canada and Australia), such as Peace Corps volunteers, teachers in international schools, diplomats, and employees of multinational corporations. And I believe that some of the colonial attitudes that I absorbed living in India are also absorbed by many, if not most, people in Great Britain and the United States, including ESL teachers. Such attitudes are part of the culture, the media, the literature, the air itself, and it is a rare person who can totally avoid or counteract them.

It is also not fair to be too judgmental, of ourselves or of others; we are all creatures of our time and place in history, and it is not necessarily fair to impose today's knowledge and standards on yesterday's attitudes. But it is important to be aware of ways in which colonial history influences us, and to grapple with these issues, both as individuals and as a profession.

Chapter 3

Tea and TESOL

*W*hen I am about eight years old, my family is on furlough from my parents' missionary work in India, and living in Vancouver. There we live in a large old house provided by the church. Along with the usual furnishings, there is an extensive set of teacups in a pretty built-in cabinet in the dining room. While we live there, my mother often hosts church women's groups to talk about missionary work. Featured at these meetings is tea served in these delicate teacups. I am thrilled when I am allowed to, very carefully, set out the cups and saucers before the "ladies" arrive. Later, as I peek into the room after a meeting has started, the image etched in my mind is that of women leaning toward each other, in a buzz of eager voices, a community of women sharing their connections over tea in these beautiful vessels, these teacups, just as so many women in so many different places throughout the world have shared their lives and concerns over tea.

My reading group is coming to my house. I clean my house and prepare light refreshments. One of the most important things I do is to choose and set out teacups from my teacup collection, along with an elegant creamer and sugar bowl.

I take pride in serving tea in these lovely china cups, and my friends enjoy sipping from them as we discuss novels by women authors, novels that often include descriptions of women drinking tea together.

The first time I take my daughter to afternoon tea, when she is about six years old, we go to the St. Francis Hotel in downtown San Francisco, on Union Square, where the fashionable stores are. She dresses up, even wearing white gloves. She enjoys her cocoa as I drink tea, and we share an assortment of tiny, exquisite sandwiches and pastries as we talk. A thoughtful pianist plays songs from musicals such as The Sound of Music *and* Mary Poppins *especially for her. It is the first of many mother-daughter teas we have shared in many cities all over the world, each of these lovely rituals providing an added memory for us to treasure.*

I do not think of myself as a collector; in fact, I pride myself on regularly going through and eliminating possessions, keeping only what I really want and need. But in fact I have several collections. Some are the obvious ones that most people have: photos, letters, family keepsakes. I still have somewhere in a box in a closet my childhood stamp collection, evoking memories of my beloved father's giving each of us four children a stamp album and regular "first day covers," and of my brothers' and my eagerly finding or buying stamps on our own and just as eagerly trading with each other. I have numerous photo albums documenting my life, my family's life, and, especially, my daughter's life. But here I focus on one special collection, one that is symbolically very important to me: my teacup collection. I explore what teacups, and tea, mean to me, and their complicated connections with my life and with my work in TESOL. They are meaningful to me in complex, layered ways, yet I also feel some ambivalence about the types of privilege they sometimes embody.

In the corner of our light-filled living room, in a beautiful cabinet with a leaded glass-paned front, sits my collection of delicate china teacups. Every time I look at them, I feel the pleasure brought on by a host of associations with some of my favorite times and places and objects: British literary novels from Jane Austen's to Barbara Pym's; British mystery novels from Agatha Christie's to Dorothy Sayers'; England itself, with its lovely green countrysides, its villages and its thatched cottages; graceful, elaborate afternoon teas in beautiful hotel lobbies and tea rooms around the world; women everywhere offering each other cups of tea and leaning toward each other over those cups as they talk about everything that matters most to them. The usual accompanying delicacies such as little sandwiches and pastries make these tea-drinking occasions, and associations, all the sweeter.

I started collecting teacups over thirty years ago, but my emotional connections with them go back to my childhood. When I grew up as a "missionary kid" in India, we always had a small afternoon meal called "tea," even when we children were too young to drink tea itself. But there was always a treat of some sort, and a certain amount of simple but important ceremony attached to the meal. It was one of the pleasures of the day, and part of the reassuring routine of our lives in this faraway but very familiar and comfortable place we lived, India.

The first vignette at the beginning of this chapter, on tea and my mother's church group, was one of my earliest introductions to the world of women's groups and gatherings, and I was fascinated by it. (See Chapter 9 for more on women's groups and communities.) Starting from that day, the custom of tea, sipped from pretty flower-patterned teacups, became forever intertwined in my mind with the idea of groups, communities, and friendships, especially those of women.

Later, when I was in an American boarding school in India, the school would provide a special afternoon tea on Sunday afternoons. Besides weak but sweet tea, we were served special sandwiches; the one I remember best and that we enjoyed most was sliced tomatoes with mayonnaise on toast; it was simple but, to us, elegant and delicious. The biggest treat of all during those boarding school years was being invited to Sunday afternoon tea at one of the teachers' apartments, or at a friend's parents' house. Because teachers and parents knew that boarding school kids were always hungry for non-institutional food, they would provide large spreads of bread and jam, cakes, cookies, and other "goodies," which we devoured with glee. So "tea" had connotations much beyond the black tea itself, connotations of being fed, nourished, treated, and indulged. And as with so many of the associations in my life, there is a literary connection here as well: these teas had further resonance because of the frequent portrayal of similar teas in the British boarding school stories that I also devoured.

We boarding school children also enjoyed a variation on the traditional Western tea and its associated customs when we would go to the nearby bazaar and buy Indian tea. We enjoyed watching the *chai wallah* make the sugary, milky tea, and then theatrically toss it high from glass to glass to cool it down.

As I got older and became the voracious reader that I have been ever since, I noticed that in so many of the novels I read, especially those by British women, whenever there was a problem to commiserate about, a triumph to celebrate, or a crisis to resolve, the characters—especially the female characters—would put the kettle on for a reassuring cup of tea. Tea in these novels—from Jane Austen's to Angela Thirkell's—seemed to be the universal prescription for any illness, any sadness, any emergency. Klinkenborg (2008) asserts, exaggerating a bit for effect, that "If you cut only the scenes that take place during tea, half of Thirkell would be missing" (p. A 18). In Austen's *Emma*, the narrator too addresses this ubiquity of tea scenes, saying about the novel's characters that "[t]hey sat down to tea—the same party around the same table—how often it had been collected!" (Austen, 1816/1957, p. 340).

During my late high school and college years, I tended to drink coffee rather than tea, perhaps thinking of tea as old-fashioned and coffee as "hip," with its associations with sitting in coffeehouses, talking about serious philosophical and political issues. But sometime after graduate school, as I began my "adult life," I rediscovered the pleasures of tea, not only the substance itself but also the ritual. Slowing down to have a cup of tea provided a peaceful oasis in the day, whether by myself or with family members or friends, whether at home or in a café or restaurant.

I started collecting teacups in my mid-twenties, soon after I set up my own household for the first time. At first I started rather accidentally, as I was given teacups by my mother and other relatives, and as I picked up a few in antique or thrift shops. At a certain point, I realized I had the beginnings of a "collection." After that, some of my friends, knowing of my interest, would give me cups for birthdays or other occasions. These gifts had special meaning because the friends who gave them shared my love of books and of community. Some of those friends were and are in the women's reading group I have been a part of for many, many years (see Chapter 9 for more about this group).

Almost all of my teacups have certain specific characteristics. First, they are made in England. Second, they are made of thin, delicate china, not the thick, practical material of the mugs more commonly used these days. Third, they are mostly decorated with floral patterns. A common motif is roses of various sizes, colors, and forms. The cups are very conventional, not avant-garde in any way. They epitomize tradition, continuity, a gentle and genteel way of life. (Those who know my left-leaning, feminist politics may be surprised at my attachment to such traditional objects and ceremonies, but to me there is no contradiction; taking time for, and valuing, community and connection are in fact both progressive and feminist ideals.) The cups are small, more appropriate for sipping than gulping. Cups and saucers always go together, and this two-part nature makes the cups, and drinking from them, seem a little frivolous, a little luxurious, rather than purely utilitarian. The beauty and fragility of the cups makes one slow down, admire, and take care with them; they seem to symbolize a statelier, more mindful way of life than we busy, modern people are usually engaged in.

I don't use my teacups frequently, but just having them on display gives me pleasure. And although I am not particularly domestic, and do not entertain frequently, I have occasionally used the teacups when friends have been at my house. The most notable such occasion was many years ago, when I hosted what I termed a "Jane Austen tea party." I invited about 15 of my friends, made and bought some of the delicacies associated with English afternoon tea, such as crustless cucumber sandwiches, small pastries, and that very English dessert, trifle. I brewed pot after pot of tea and served it in my special teacups. The party was quite a success, and to this day, friends tell me how much they remember it and enjoyed it.

One of my favorite ways to celebrate a special occasion, whether it be a birthday, a reunion with old friends, or the holidays, is to go to afternoon tea at an elegant hotel or tearoom. Just recently, a colleague and I took another colleague to tea for her birthday, and she repeatedly told us how it made her feel cherished and celebrated. Everything lends itself to celebration of occasions and of friendships: the beautiful hotel lobby, the exquisite teapots and teacups and the accompanying paraphernalia (tea strainer, silver teaspoons, china or silver creamer and sugar bowls, tea cozies), the fragrant black tea itself (often with names that evoke my childhood in India, such as Darjeeling, Assam, and Nilgiri), the descriptions of the tea on the elaborate, ornately scripted menu, the tiered tray with the dainty treats that accompany the tea (scones, crumpets, Devonshire cream, lemon curd, tiny cakes and shortbread—all are both delicious and reminiscent of the many tea scenes in my favorite British novels), quiet conversation, and unhurried, lovely, attentive service. Anyone would feel pampered and happy surrounded by these elements!

Sometimes I fear that this enjoyable, life-affirming tradition is becoming a thing of the past. Some months ago, I bought a cup and saucer at a hip, urban store in an affluent area. When I approached the cashier, a young woman of perhaps twenty, she turned in perplexity to her equally young colleague, asking whether she should charge me for one piece or two. The other young woman replied that "the cup and the *plate* [sic] go together." Clearly the custom of drinking afternoon tea from cups and saucers was not one that these young women were familiar with. When one goes to tea at a hotel, often the average age of the other tea drinkers is quite high. And in another ominous sign, two of the big hotels in my city that traditionally served afternoon tea on weekdays have stopped doing so.

Yet as long as little girls still have tea parties with their tea sets, the ritual of tea and the way that tea symbolizes connection and conversation will continue. I recently opened the comics page of my local newspaper and found that Lynn Johnston, creator of the comic strip "For Better or Worse," had included a two-day storyline on a little girl coming to terms with her father's plans to remarry. The stepmother-to-be asks the little girl, "Francie . . . could we have a chat? Woman to woman?" and the girl replies "Would you like some tea?" They proceed to carry out an important conversation—and some female bonding—over pretend cups of tea, using the little girl's tea set (Johnston, 2008, p. E6). (Granted, Johnston is Canadian, and as Canada is a British Commonwealth country, it preserves more of Britain's customs than the United States does.)

As my stories illustrate, afternoon tea, with all its paraphernalia and rituals, is very much a gendered experience. If one looks around any hotel lobby or tearoom where this meal is served, one will see, almost exclusively, women and girls. I have gone to tea with my mother, my daughter, my nieces, my research group, my writing group, and other colleagues and friends, all female, but never with a man. My daughter once wanted to share her love of afternoon hotel teas with her boyfriend at the time, but although he was polite about it, he obviously did not enjoy it as she and I do. Perhaps it is considered by men as a non-serious meal, or a meal that focuses too much on sweet delicacies rather than hearty food. Perhaps its connotations are too feminine, too "girly" or "frou-frou." Perhaps it is too obviously a way for groups of women to connect, to treat themselves, to talk, to share a little respite from their busy lives. It is hard to explain without resorting to generalizations, but for whatever reasons, the ritual of afternoon tea, and drinking from teacups, has very feminine associations for many people. (I do note, however, that tea itself, and taking a break from work for tea, is common for men as well as women throughout many parts of the world.)

My one discomfort with going somewhere that provides a formal tea service is that it is clearly a symbol of a certain kind of privilege. In order to enjoy tea at a luxurious hotel, one must have both the resources to pay for this rather expensive treat and the leisure time to enjoy it. As an "extra" meal, it does not have the utilitarian function that even an expensive lunch or dinner does; on the surface, at least, the meal of afternoon tea seems to be an added, entirely unnecessary luxury. Although I believe in sharing tea and food as a way of bonding with family members and friends, of building and cementing community, I acknowledge the privilege that is necessary to indulge in such formal teas.

The social class aspect of formal afternoon tea is illustrated by Henry James, in the opening scene of *The Portrait of a Lady* (1881/1983), when the narrator opines that "Under certain circumstances there are few hours in life more agreeable than the hour dedicated to the ceremony known as afternoon tea," (p. 1), and goes on to describe those circumstances as follows:

> The implements of the little feast had been disposed upon the lawn of an old English country house, in what I should call the perfect middle of a splendid summer afternoon . . . the scene expressed that sense of leisure still to come which is perhaps the chief source of one's enjoyment of such a scene at such an hour. (p. 1)

Note the country house, the lawn, and the access to leisure time, all signs of social class privilege.

This social class privilege also intersects with racial privilege; in general, at least in the United States, it has been white people who partake of tea in the more expensive and luxurious settings of elegant hotels and tearooms. In such venues, it is common to see that the servers are mostly people of color, while the customers are mostly white. In the deference of the servers and the seeming entitlement of those being served, it is hard not to avoid acknowledging echoes of the privileged being served by the less privileged throughout history, and the common thread of racial and class overtones of such relationships.

Tea also, and relatedly, has connotations of colonial privilege. Tea was and is grown in such once-colonized countries as India, Sri Lanka, and Kenya, often for export to Western countries; the workers on the tea plantations often labor for little pay and under less than optimal working conditions. Many of the British colonials in countries around the world preserved this ritual of British life, wherever they were, with the added "luxury" of having Indian or African servants serving them. Kuwahara (2004) states that "the ritual of drinking tea provides an ironic commentary on the theme of property and power" (n.p.). The same tea scenes I have mentioned from British novels set in England also occurred in British novels set in the colonies, such as E. M. Forster's *Passage to India* (1924/1952) and some of Somerset Maugham's stories set in Singapore and elsewhere. De Albuquerque (1998), in a fascinating description of all the large and small matters shared by those who grew up in countries colonized by the British, says that

> One was (is) always assured when visiting other marginalized ex-colonials all over that world that . . . afternoon tea would (will) be familiar. . . . [It] had its assemblage of prescribed foods—scones and clotted cream, . . . shortbread (Walker's), and finger sandwiches, the most recognizable being cucumber. (n.p.)

I have a complicated relationship with notions of colonial privilege. My political and social views condemn many, perhaps most, aspects of colonialism. Yet because I grew up as the child of missionary parents in India, soon after the country became independent, I was indirectly implicated in colonialism, or at least the remnants of colonialism. And because like many children, I feel nostalgic for my childhood and its accompanying experiences, artifacts, and memories, I am emotionally drawn to cultural practices and artifacts with some roots in colonialism. There is something deeply embedded in my history and psyche that draws me to portrayals of colonial situations, particularly in India but also elsewhere. Intellectually I condemn the negative aspects of colonial rule and power, yet emotionally—almost at a cellular level—I experience a vivid sense memory, a deep connection to scenes of contact between the colonizer and the colonized, scenes that evoke my childhood, my earliest memories, and my complex yearnings. I am profoundly ambivalent about these feelings, and it is both painful and liberating to write about them as I am doing here.

Tea is just one example of my connection to this colonial legacy. Others include the British novels I mention in this chapter, many taking place in or alluding to Great Britain's colonial outposts around the world. In addition, those who worked on tea plantations in the past, and sometimes those who work on them even now, have often been exploited. Jane Austen, for example, although often accused of writing only about small town life, courtship, and marriage, was well aware of the slave labor that produced tea and other goods that her genteel characters consumed, and made at least oblique mention of these topics in her novels, most notably in *Mansfield Park* (1814/1964). The father of the family at Mansfield Park, Sir Thomas Bertram, has made his fortune largely from his plantations in the West Indies, and during the course of the novel, goes there to check on and shore up his business interests. In a telling scene, the main character, Fanny, asks Sir Thomas about slavery and is answered by a "dead silence" (p. 182). Many critics (e.g., Southam, 1995; White, 2006) have argued that in *Mansfield Park* there is a subtext of criticism of slavery and its part in supporting the Bertram family's lifestyle. Austen knew about plantations in Antigua, particularly through her own father's friendship with a plantation owner there, and knew of the horrors of slavery through her brother Francis, who was in the Navy and who wrote opposing slavery. She herself was known to read abolitionist literature, including her favorite poet Cowper's critiques of slavery, and to support the abolition of slavery.

Postcolonial scholars have written of tea's connection to colonialism. Chatterjee (2001) writes that tea

> becomes a medium through which the chronicles
> of global expansion and conquest can be told. . . .
> From the late sixteenth century, tea titillated Euro-
> pean palates, by virtue of its consummate connec-
> tion to the riches of the celestial kingdom itself:
> the secret and shadow empire of the great
> "Orient." (p. 21)

Chatterjee (2001) also points out the gendered nature of the labor of picking tea, as many of those picking tea were and are women. Thus, once again, we see the intertwining of types of privilege, or lack of privilege, in this case related to both social class and gender, as the wealthier Europeans drink tea produced by the labor of the poorer tea workers, who also bear the burden of gender oppression.

My ambivalence about my relationship to the colonial legacy also plays out in my professional life, in my ESOL classrooms, where I am very aware of social class, privilege, race, and colonial vestiges. Not only my life but also my teaching sometimes seems implicated in the colonial legacy I have experienced through growing up in India as a "missionary kid," through my connections with England and Canada, and through my predilection for British literature and customs. (See Chapter 2 for a fuller discussion of the colonial legacy I have experienced in my personal and professional lives.) Tea may or may not be an immediate part of that legacy in professional contexts, yet my mind often turns to it as connected to my relationships with my teaching and my students.

Many ESOL students, of course, come from countries with their own traditions of drinking tea, and their own ceremonies and associations with tea drinking. The well-known Japanese tea ceremony is just one example. Tea is also grown in some of their countries, which brings up the issues of who owns the tea plantations, who works there, and how workers are treated. In the past, our associations might be, as Chatterjee (2001) and others have pointed out, that rich white Westerners paid for and drank tea produced by poor non-white non-Westerners by the sweat of their brows, under exploitative conditions; these notions had, and have, much truth to them. However, the situation has always been, and is now more than ever, much more complicated. Even when I was in India, and saw tea plantations as we drove up the *ghat* (a rough, winding road) to our boarding school in the Palni Hills, I knew that the owners of the plantations were now Indian, and some of their children attended the same school as I did. Those children came from India's upper middle class, the business class; children of the workers who picked and processed the tea could not afford to attend our school. So social class became, after Indian Independence, a stronger factor than colonial hierarchies. That situation from India reminds me of the situation of the international students in ESOL classes at my university; these students who can afford to study in the United States and elsewhere are more likely to be children of the tea plantation owners than of the workers who pick and process the tea. Our ESOL students at times experience racial and ethnic prejudice, but also, conversely, benefit from their often very privileged social class positions. As I discussed in my 1995 article on privilege, these students often carry much more social class privilege than most people from their countries, or for that matter most people from the United States, including most of their ESOL instructors.

Again, this matter of social class privilege is often the cause for ambivalence about my roles and relationships with my students. On the one hand, sharing the "gift" of the English language, with all the implications of "my" language being superior, puts me in a position of a condescending colonial dispenser of good things to the "natives." (See Chapter 2 for more on this notion.) On the other hand, most of the actual students in my university ESL classes are very privileged, well-traveled, sophisticated, and (although they are generally very polite and appreciative) in no way seem to feel that they are passively, gratefully receiving my beneficent instruction in the ways of those with power. Some of them are as likely as I am to have dined or taken tea in the great hotels of the world; many of them have servants at home who bring them tea in the morning or on demand. When I recently taught a "restaurant" unit in one of my classes, using restaurant reviews and guides as readings, I found that many of the students had eaten at—and drunk tea at—the most expensive restaurants in our restaurant-obsessed city, San Francisco. The issue is, of course, not just one of wealth and experience, but of privilege. Many international students in the United States and other Western countries are quite privileged, and although they may experience some cultural adjustments, do not feel inferior or inadequate in Western settings; in other words, the remnants of colonialism are disappearing, at least for this privileged class of ESOL students. I do not often teach immigrant students, who are generally less privileged, but I know that they are more likely to experience being treated in a condescending or even hostile manner. So I am not proclaiming that colonial attitudes, racism, and other forms of prejudice and discrimination do not still exist; of course they do. But the sands are shifting, the boundaries are more porous, and relationships and interactions among ESOL students, their American classmates, and their instructors are more complex than ever.

Very recently, one of my star ESOL students from the semester before, a young man from China, presented me with two canisters of excellent Chinese green tea. To him, the tea represented his country and culture. He was thanking me for my teaching, but also sharing his culture, and all the connotations of tea drinking that we both recognized: taking time for nourishment and the small pleasures of life, sharing social and communal moments.

Another recent moment that reminded me of the complexities of colonialism and culture came when I heard and saw outside my office window a group of Indian and Pakistani students playing an improvised game of cricket on the lawn between the Arts building and the ornate, towering Catholic church on our campus. As they laughed and cheered each other on, on that unseasonably sunny January day, I savored the memories of similar scenes in both India and England, and I savored as well the interweaving of cultures, languages, religions, and interests that such a scene symbolized. Yes, cricket is that most British of games, yet it has long been taken up by Indians and those of many other nationalities and ethnicities with enthusiasm, and here it was being played in the United States on a lawn more often the scene of touch football or Frisbee games, not to mention graduation receptions. (See Joseph O'Neill's 2008 novel *Netherland* for a lovely, complex rendering of the significance of cricket to many immigrants to the United States and the joy that they take from playing the game.)

These shifts in the social landscapes of the world are proof that the world is changing, that some of the old paradigms of power and privilege are breaking up. In my ESOL classes, I see that time moves on, that symbols change their meanings, and that healing happens. The colonial and even postcolonial years and relationships are evolving. My students today, even from countries and cultures that were colonized or oppressed or discriminated against in various ways, have a sense of confidence and a sense of their rightful place in the world that no longer fits the old paradigms. We in TESOL can rejoice in these changes, and in the part we may have in promoting such change and in assisting our students to take advantage of their opportunities to be educated citizens of the world. The tea that my Chinese student presented to me has a very different meaning than the tea that was served to me by the Indian *chai wallahs* of my childhood. The children of those *chai wallahs* are, perhaps, now the scientists and entrepreneurs at leading universities and companies around the world.

Yet I am very aware of the fact that the positive shifts away from colonial power do not change the basic condition that unfair privilege and lack of privilege still exist, whether determined by social class, gender, race, or other factors. We educators, especially ESOL educators, need to be mindful of all that has gone before, and of all that has changed and is changing in our world and the worlds of our students, but also of all the injustices that still need to be addressed.

And so I come back to tea, with all its complex meanings for me, and perhaps for others who read this. Tea is an example of how the elements of our everyday material lives are so important, both in themselves and symbolically. Tea brings with it so many personal and literary associations, and forms part of my web of connections to other people, places, times, and cultures. Although my enjoyment of tea, and teacups, and the rituals of drinking tea with friends at home or in lovely hotel restaurants, is complicated by the knowledge of the various types of privilege inherent in these experiences, there is a part of me too that wants to simply and uncomplicatedly enjoy the steaming, fragrant tea, the ceremony of drinking tea, the accouterments, the beloved teacups, the company and community of drinking tea and eating together, and the pause in one's life to talk, to commiserate, to celebrate life together. My ambivalent relationship with tea and all its rituals and meanings echoes in some sense the complex and fraught history of tea, its production and consumption, and its connotations of privilege.

Chapter 4

Shifting Sites, Shifting Identities: A 30-Year Perspective[1]

Note to the Reader:

Because I have taught at the same institution my whole career, and because so much of what I write about in this book is closely related to, and influenced by, my experiences at that institution, I include this previously published piece about the power of institutions in our teaching and writing lives. This essay focuses on the changes my program and institution have undergone during the 30-plus years I have taught there. I use the changes at my institution as a lens to examine changes in our field and factors that affect the way ESOL and second language education are viewed and treated within academe. Publishing this piece felt a bit risky to me, as I describe both negative and positive aspects of my experiences and of the institution;

---

[1]   This essay is a very slightly revised version of one that was originally published as Vandrick, S. (2006). Shifting sites, shifting identities: A thirty-year perspective. In P. K. Matsuda, C. Ortmeier-Hooper, & X. You (Eds.), *Politics of second language writing: In search of the promised land* (pp. 280–293). West Lafayette, IN: Parlor Press.

this sense of riskiness was mainly allayed by the fact that most of the negative aspects pertained to my early years at the institution, and most of the positive aspects relate to more recent years, up to and including the present. Now I am proud to be a faculty member at my institution, and feel fortunate in my situation there, but am also well aware of the types of privilege that allow me to be in this position.

To highlight the importance of the institutions where we do our work, and as an illustration of some of the social and political issues that arise in institutions where second language writing programs are housed, here I tell the story of my institution, the University of San Francisco (USF), where I have been a faculty member for the 30-plus years that the ESL program has existed there. Here I describe the many changes the program has undergone, and the contexts, causes and consequences of those changes. In those 30-plus years, the ESL writing program, along with the rest of the ESL program, has had five different names and structures, including several changes in affiliation and reporting line: it has been an independent program, an academic department, and a part of a larger academic department; it has ranged from being entirely disconnected from the L1 writing program to being part of the same department. These changes have taken place within, and been greatly affected by, the context of larger changes within the university, including curricular changes, faculty unionization, major shifts in university administration, dramatic ebbs and flows in the number and types of international students enrolled, and emphatic changes in the mission and goals of the university. Further, the changes have taken place in the context of larger changes in the TESOL profession.

I would like to note here that although this is an essay about the shifting sites and identities of ESL within the larger institution, my own professional history is so intertwined with the story of the program that I cannot clearly separate one story from the other; thus my chapter is at least partially a narrative, with elements of a personal narrative. (For a more personal version of parts of this story, see Chapter 8.) Note that—as part of a move against limiting the definition of research to quantitative, experimental research paradigms—personal narrative (including teacher narratives) has become an increasingly common and accepted mode of inquiry in academe, and in particular in composition studies (Fontaine & Hunter, 1993; Hindman, 2003; Roen, Brown, & Enos, 1999; Trimmer, 1997). Narratives provide some of the same kinds of data that ethnographic research, case studies, interviews, and diary studies provide. (For further discussion of the place of personal narrative in scholarly writing, please see Casanave & Schecter, 1997; Casanave & Vandrick, 2003a; Connelly & Clandinin, 1999; Haroian-Guerin, 1999; Ritchie & Wilson, 2000). Here it is my intention, however, to contextualize the story in a larger framework, and I hope that this essay thereby sheds light on connections between individual stories and institutional stories, and on the implications of these stories for the future of ESL, and ESL writing, at our institutions.

The History

I will begin with a brief history of ESL and ESL writing at USF, then will list relevant factors influencing that history, and will go on to outline some of the implications of the various stages and sites the program has gone through.

The ESL program was initially established at the University of San Francisco in 1974, and was essentially an Intensive English Program that enrolled both matriculated and nonmatriculated students. It was called the English Language Center, and was set up as an independent program that was led by an administrative director who reported to the Vice President for Academic Affairs. The program had little connection to the rest of the university.

In the second year of the program, the full-time faculty were moved from term appointments to tenure-track appointments, an important improvement in the status of the faculty and the program, and one that was to make a critical difference.

Although the enrollment was large and the program was academically and financially successful, there was much political turmoil that led to a change in directors and to the renaming of the program, in 1976, as the World English Center. In 1979, the center was rehoused in the College of Arts and Sciences and the administration-appointed director reported to the Dean of that College.

A few difficult years of further turmoil later, the university decided to limit international student enrollment, and serve only matriculated students. At that point when the program was, for the first time, *not* an intensive program, the university in 1985 renamed it once again, this time as the Intensive English Program.

During this time period, there were many difficulties and skirmishes between the administration and the faculty, especially about workload. Although the ESL faculty was technically declared equal to other faculty at the university, the administration both at the program level and at the university-wide level resisted according ESL faculty the same status and working conditions as "real" faculty. For one example, the ESL faculty were required to teach many more hours than other faculty did; one Dean at the time justified this decision by stating that ESL faculty did not have to do any preparation, but merely walked into class, opened a grammar book, and taught. Worse, several faculty members were fired. Others who stayed were repeatedly denied tenure and then promotion. It was only with the support of the new Faculty Association—a union (more about this later)—that any of the faculty (in some cases only after extended appeal and arbitration processes) kept or were reinstated to their positions and were, eventually, tenured and promoted. However, many more were never reinstated, and to this day there are far fewer full-time faculty members than there were during the first years.

A few long years later, in 1992, with more changes in administration, and in particular with the appointment of a supportive new Dean of Arts and Sciences, the program became the ESL Department. This change was a real turning point, and was enormous in its implications. It recognized that the ESL program and faculty were equal and equivalent to other disciplines and faculty on campus, and should therefore have the same department status as, for example, History, Biology, or Sociology. This new status allowed the faculty to elect a chairperson and control the curriculum, policies, and budget of the department, rather than being directed by administrators.

The last change (to date)—the fifth name, site, and status—occurred in 1999, when the dean asked the ESL faculty to consider the possibility of becoming part of a newly forming department, Communication Studies. This department would combine the Communication major, the ESL program, and the L1 writing program (which up to this point had been called the Expository Writing Program, but soon became the Rhetoric and Composition program). Although there were some political and personnel-related reasons for this proposed change, the primary reason was that such a department structure would facilitate much closer coordination and articulation among the three related programs, and would allow for curricular connections and innovations. The three programs would continue to have much autonomy, but would also work together as a department.

After much discussion, all three units agreed to this new departmental structure. (Note that the fact that the faculty was consulted at all was a huge improvement from the earlier years of the ESL program's existence.) The ESL faculty reasoned that although in joining the larger department we would lose some of the independence we had enjoyed as a separate department, we would gain in strength, clout, and status. And although there have been some rough spots in establishing the new department, overall it has in fact turned out to be a successful and productive situation, and we look forward to even more collaboration and mutually beneficial curricular and other projects.

As a sign of the ESL program's equal role in the new department, let me note that in 2002 the coordinator of the ESL division was elected by the Communication Studies department faculty as its new Chair, and in

2005, she was elected to another term. A senior member of the campus faculty, whose having served as Chair of the Arts Council and in other positions of leadership within the college and university had enhanced her credibility and visibility within the university, she was recognized by all in the department to be doing an outstanding job as Chair, one who was actively instrumental in promoting and facilitating cooperation among the three units.

Other Relevant Factors in This Story

There are several relevant factors that were involved in the program faculty's ability to make these last two positive changes in our position, status, and effectiveness at the university: the first change being becoming a department, and the second change being becoming stronger through joining a larger department. The most important of these change-promoting factors are as follows.

1. Unionization

First and probably foremost in importance is the fact that the faculty at the university became unionized in 1975. This was a long, hard fight, with many difficult consequences, but it was necessary and beneficial for faculty, and therefore for the atmosphere and quality of the university. The unionization came at a very good time for the ESL program and faculty: although it also intensified the already existing acrimony between faculty and administration, and led to many terribly difficult years, the union with its processes and protections was able to preserve the full-time tenure track positions in ESL, and helped to make—eventually—the ESL faculty's working conditions approach equality with other faculty's. I would also like to point out that much later the university's part-time faculty—including the ESL part-time instructors—also unionized, and were able to earn many protections, including a sort of modified tenure called the "preferred hiring pool," along with much-improved pay and some medical and other benefits.

I know that some academics do not approve of unions for faculty, but I believe that when working under difficult and unfair administrations, unions provide the only way to balance, at least somewhat, the power equation. In our case, the status of our program and its faculty would be far lower if it were not for the union.

2. Changes in administration

The second most important factor in the ESL program's progress was changes in the university administration, most notably the appointment of a new Dean of the College of Arts and Sciences who came from the faculty and had been active in the Faculty Association (the union). He had initially been appointed by the university administration as Acting Dean. Before a search for a more permanent Dean was launched, a compelling majority of the College faculty—including the ESL faculty—signed a petition and wrote letters strongly requesting that he be retained as Dean. The administration, clearly somewhat surprised by this display of near-unanimity, acquiesced. This event was a strong indication both of the power of the faculty under the union, and of the administration's graceful realization that it was more productive to work with the faculty than to maintain an adversarial relationship.

This new Dean was the first senior administrator at USF who treated the ESL program and faculty as equal to other programs and faculties. He was the one who facilitated our becoming an academic department, with a faculty chair. He also reduced our teaching load to match other faculty's, procured us private offices (finally!), and encouraged and supported our research and other academic and professional activities.

Please take a moment to imagine the difference it makes to have a senior administrator who supports your work and takes it as a given that you should be treated like any other program and faculty. And as trivial as it sounds to those who have fortunately been able to take these things for granted, imagine how it feels to finally—after many years—have access to travel and research funds, and to have a decent private office, with one's own computer, telephone, windows, and lock on the door!

3. University's shifting stance on internationalism and multiculturalism

Another important change was the university's shifting stance on internationalism and multiculturalism. In the mid-1970s, the university had one of the largest proportions of international students of any university; in addition, because of its location in the multicultural San Francisco Bay area, there were many students from a multiplicity of ethnic backgrounds, particularly Asian. Some of the university's traditional constituencies (especially among the alumni and the Board of Trustees) were concerned that the university was becoming *too* diverse; the university administration apparently agreed, and drastically cut the number of international students it enrolled. In other words, the university at that time did not really see international and immigrant students—at least as such a large proportion of the enrolled students—as an asset. However, in the past 10–15 years, the university has—to its credit—evidenced a huge turnaround in its attitude, now seeing and strongly emphasizing the benefits of a diverse student population. One of the official strategic initiatives, according to the university catalog, is to "Enroll, support and graduate a diverse student body" (University of San Francisco Catalog, 2005–2007, p. 5). And in 2004 and 2005 the university president announced with pride that USF was listed in the *Princeton Review* as one of the most diverse universities in the country. This change in the university's stance was partly a response to the changing times, partly a function of USF's location in the liberal San Francisco Bay area, partly a sign of the Jesuit Society's increasing commitment to social activism, and partly a natural consequence of the College's recent hiring of several cohorts of progressive young faculty members. Thus the ESL program and the way it has been regarded within the university has fallen and risen with the changing goals and focuses of the university.

I believe this is an important point to look at when examining the shifting locuses and statuses of ESL and L2 writing programs, and I believe that my institution—like other institutions—has historically devalued international and minority students; clearly one of the reasons that ESL is marginalized is this very devaluation of "Others." This kind of ethnocentrism is harmful not only to the students who are Othered, and to the programs that serve them, but to the larger institution as well (Benesch, 2001; Canagarajah, 2002; Morgan, 1998). It is fortunate that the situation has much improved, at my institution and at others, but TESOL professionals must be vigilant, especially in these post–September 11th days of increased U.S. government suspicion of people from outside the United States, and of people from non-Western cultures and non-Christian religions.

4. University's increasing focus on social justice

Closely related to the university's commitment to diversity, especially during the past 10 to 15 years, is its increasing emphasis and focus on a commitment to social justice. When the university's Mission and Goals were revised a few years ago, the new statement included the following: "The University will distinguish itself as a diverse, socially responsible learning community" (University of San Francisco catalog, 2005–2007, p. 4), and one of the goals listed was "social responsibility in fulfilling the University's mission" (p. 5); the new tagline on all the university's publicity was "Educating minds and hearts to change the world." This emphasis on social responsibility and social justice has also reinforced the ESL program's place in the university, especially as the program has enrolled students from struggling countries or backgrounds. For example, when the Dalai Lama recently came to be honored by, and speak to, the USF community, a Tibetan student in our ESL program was prominently involved in the ceremonies and publicity surrounding the event.

5. Changing enrollment profile

Also evolving has been the enrollment profile of the ESL Program. In the early years of the program, by far the majority of ESL students were Intensive English Program (IEP) students who had come specifically to study English. With time, a much larger proportion of the students consisted of matriculated students, and now matriculated students form the majority. Because matriculated students are much more connected to the mainstream of the university, taking classes in various departments, interacting with American students, and of course staying much longer, this trend has also promoted the visibility and status of the ESL program on the campus.

6. Credit for ESL classes

A related development is that after many years of ESL faculty's and students' fighting for students' receiving academic credit for ESL classes, a few years ago this credit was approved by the university. Up to eight credits of students' ESL classes (most commonly, ESL writing classes) count toward degree credit, and all grades in ESL classes, even beyond the eight credits, are averaged into students' grade point averages. This development makes everyone—students, faculty, and administration—take the ESL classes more seriously.

7. Flexibility offered by a smaller university

Another factor that has helped the program is that, because the university is not large (about 4,800 undergraduates and 3,200 graduate students), there is a flexibility that allows and even promotes interdisciplinary research, teaching, and service. This atmosphere has allowed ESL faculty to be closely involved in the committee work and other administrative structures of the university; to teach non-ESL classes in other departments and even other colleges as appropriate; and to work on research and otherwise engage intellectually and academically with other faculty and other disciplinary units on campus. This, again, promotes the visibility and status of the ESL faculty and thus of the program.

When the ESL faculty joined the Communication Studies Department, this moving beyond disciplinary borders was accelerated. ESL faculty—both full- and part-time—have frequently taught public speaking, writing, and linguistics courses in the Communication and Rhetoric/Composition divisions, and often consult on curriculum and policies. In particular, the ESL and Rhetoric/Composition divisions have been able to work closely together on improving the teaching of writing at the university. They have also been able to work together on improving the status of the faculty and of the programs. For example, faculty from one unit frequently serve on another unit's faculty search committees.

8. Individual faculty members' efforts

An eighth and final factor involved in the ESL program's ability to move forward has been the efforts of individual faculty members. When given the opportunity and encouragement by the new, supportive Dean, faculty members welcomed the opportunity to prove the ESL faculty and programs deserving of the equality finally being granted to them. They—we—saw that we could one by one, by hard work, convince our fellow faculty, administrators, and others that the TESOL discipline was in fact a legitimate one, and that its faculty were as capable as any faculty of producing high quality research and publications, and of doing their share of the service work of the university. Every time our new publications were listed in the university newsletter, every time one of us chaired a committee or council, every time one of us got a campus award, we felt we were doing so not only for ourselves as individuals, but for the program, the discipline, and the profession.

Our fellow faculty throughout the college and university have responded very positively to us, inviting us to join them in various ways. I, for example, have taught classes in Women's Studies and Women's Literature (invited by the English Department), and at one point directed USF's Women's Studies program. At another point I directed USF's combined undergraduate/graduate teacher preparation/credentialing program. A colleague has taught Linguistics classes in the Communication division, as well as teacher education classes in the School of Education, and has been a member of the president's budget committee and other high-level university-wide committees. For another example of cross-disciplinary connections, I belong to a reading/writing group of women faculty—from fields such as History, Sociology, Media Studies, and French—who read and discuss feminist and other theory, and who discuss our research and writing projects with each other. (See Chapter 9 for more on this group.)

Implications for Identity Construction of Program, Faculty, and Students

Now I would like to examine more closely ways in which the changes in names, sites, and structures have affected the ways that the program, faculty, and students construct their identities and perceive their roles and statuses within the university, and how they are perceived by others at the institution.

1. Identity construction of the ESL/L2 writing discipline

As readers know, ESL, and ESL writing, have often been, like L1 writing programs, considered by many to be less rigorous, less prestigious, less "real" academic disciplines than long-established areas such as English Literature, Economics, and Political Science. (See Rose, 1985, for one of many discussions of L1 composition's marginalization, and of writing instruction being characterized as "remediation.") This is partly because these are relatively new disciplines, and partly because they are considered "service" areas rather than "content" areas.

As Linda Lonon Blanton (2002) has so vividly put it regarding ESL writing, and as I think applies to ESL as a whole as well,

> In truth, ESL composition, like a foster child, has been hard to 'place' . . . college program administrators have created jerry-rigged curricular constructs that perch second language students precariously between institutional units, both in and out of the academic mainstream. (p. 152)

In fact, ESL writing has been further marginalized not only within institutions, but when it is included as part of L1 composition programs, has often been marginalized there as well. So too have the L2 students themselves, who are generally taught by part-time and in some cases inexperienced (in ESL) faculty, as Jessica Williams (1995) and others have noted. Williams and others further note that ESL writing classes are considered "remedial," a label that has long ensured the separation and marginalization of ESL classes and students.

I don't pretend to say that this perception has changed completely at my university or in general, but I do think that much progress has been made. Some progress has been made at specific institutions such as mine; some has been made at the level of the profession and its professional organizations and publications. For examples of the latter: Tony Silva, Ilona Leki, Paul Kei Matsuda, and others have worked hard to establish second language writing as a respected area of study, a field of its own, through the Symposium on Second Language Writing held every other year at Purdue University, through the *Journal of Second Language Writing*, and through other publications and forums. They have also reached out to the L1 composition profession and community through joining committees of, and organizing panels and giving papers at, such organizations as College Composition and Communication (CCC) and its annual conference (CCCC).

2. Identity construction of ESL faculty

The promotion of the status of the discipline and that of the faculty reinforce each other. As Elsa Auerbach so strongly put it, "A fact of life for ESL educators is that we are marginalized" (1991, p. 1). At my institution, there was initial strong resistance (from the administration and even from other faculty on campus) to granting equitable working conditions, tenure, and promotions to ESL faculty; it was only with the gradual improvement of the status of the program, the support of certain administrators who believed in equity and believed in the ESL faculty, and some hard work, that the faculty reached the position of being judged by their peers and by the administration to be deserving of tenure and promotion and other signs of academic acceptance and equity.

3. Identity construction of ESL students

Also closely related are the ways in which our ESL students' sites and identities are regarded and constructed within the institution. According to Blanton (2002), "ESL students—whether international or resident—don't understand how the system works or how and why they end up placed where they do. No wonder" (p. 152). Certainly the widely varying sites and organizational structures, and the sometimes unclear relationships among them, have often been confusing, alienating, and even sometimes humiliating for students.

Fortunately—but only after a painfully long period of time—at my institution, the status of international students, and in particular students in ESL and ESL writing classes, has risen throughout the years as the status of the program has risen. In the early years, the program, like many ESL programs, was considered to be separate from the mainstream of the university, a program that was housed there but was not very connected to the rest of the university. Students themselves felt this separation. As the program gained legitimacy and status, and as the university's attitude toward the value of international and multicultural students and diversity became more positive, the position of ESL students rose as well.

In addition, students have benefited pedagogically, and can now see, much more than in the past, that the L1 and L2 writing programs are integrated, that the faculty of each talk to and consult with each other and back each other up on decisions about, for example, placement.

Focus on L1/L2 parallels

I would like to focus briefly on the parallels between the evolution of the status of the L1 and L2 writing programs at USF (and at many other institutions). Both have been regarded by many as "service units" and as less than completely legitimate disciplines. Both have—in the past—been more closely controlled by administration and had less faculty control over their work than have other disciplines. Both have endured criticism from other university faculty for not preparing students adequately for the writing tasks they face during their university studies (see Janopoulos, 1992; and Zamel, 1995, 1996, among others, on this latter point). In both cases, the situation has improved at USF, because of the factors I have listed, and because the two disciplines/ programs have recently worked more closely together in the new shared department structure; the two programs/disciplines have been able to lend each other strength, support, and legitimacy. As Paul Kei Matsuda (1998, 1999, 2003) and others have pointed out, the two disciplines have historically diverged in most institutions, and as disciplines, but certainly should be working more closely together both at the institutional level and across the professions.

Conclusion

Although each program's situation is different, I believe that there are some common threads in my story that may resonate for others at other institutions, and I hope that some of those threads have been evident in this chapter. I hope that I don't convey here an overly optimistic and perhaps naïve attitude about the situation of ESL and ESL writing in academe. I cannot and will not ever forget the obstacles and problems that we dealt with in our institution, and that so many ESL and ESL writing programs have dealt with and are still dealing with in their academic homes. But I do believe that with time and effort, our still young field is establishing itself, and can and will continue to establish itself, as a legitimate, essential discipline that will continue to grow in status and influence in the future. Those of us who believe in and care passionately about our profession and our students can and will make it happen.

Chapter 5

Fathers and Mentors

A copy of the journal containing my first major publication arrives in the *mail. I feel both joy and a twinge of sadness; it has been a long, difficult journey to this point. I tell my husband and daughter, and my closest colleagues, and they are all happy for me. But the ones I really want to tell, and show the article to, are my parents, especially my father. I call to tell them, and they are gratifyingly excited for me. I put a copy of the article in the mail to them, and a few days later I get a call from my dad, telling me he has read my article, likes it very much, and is proud of me. He mentions some specific points in the article, showing me he has read it carefully and thoughtfully. I am so pleased to have made him proud, and so grateful to have his unwavering care, love, and support.*

Soon after Stanley Nel becomes our new Dean, he meets with the full-time faculty of our program. He listens carefully to our concerns about the way we, and our program, have been treated under former and current administrators. He is very quick to understand our situation, and promises to look into matters, and to rectify inequities. It is strange and wonderful to have an administrator who actu-

ally listens, treats us with respect, and is genuinely committed to improving the situation. As part of the conversation, he asks us our opinion about our institution's entrance policies for international students. There is an instant of shock, as we have never been asked by other administrators about that, or about anything else that indicated recognition of our expertise in TESOL. It is a small but telling moment, one that shows us change has finally come, and one that I will never forget.

We are all creatures of our formative influences, especially our parents, both our personal (biological, adopted, or substitute) parents, and our academic "parents." I have been fortunate to have terrific, loving, generous, thoughtful parents who have always been actively engaged in my life, yet without being judgmental or interfering. I naïvely assumed the world would be like that—like them—and looked for the same qualities in my bosses/supervisors. In some cases I was right, in others not. I have been appalled by, and have felt betrayed and let down by, some dreadful bosses; in other cases, I have been very fortunate in supervisors and mentors. Some of my academic "fathers" have been strong forces in my academic career. Some have been my professors, some my supervisors, some my mentors, and some a combination of these; some have been theorists/scholars whose ideas have influenced me and my work; all have taught me, helped me, and supported me in various ways. It is these academic fathers, along with my actual father, that I celebrate in this essay.

I want to note here that I also have a wonderful mother, and have had some excellent female supervisors and colleagues as well, one in particular who has been a longtime colleague, friend, and supporter; I have written about and will write about my mother, Norrie Vandrick, and these colleagues and mentors as well, elsewhere (e.g., see Chapter 9 for discussion of many of my supportive colleagues, mostly women). I will just note here, however, that I acknowledge that there is a gendered aspect to the differences in my relationships with my "mothers" (who, except for my actual mother, are more like sisters) and my relationships with my "fathers." This was probably, at least in part, because early in my career, most of the people in positions of power in academe were men; this was and is most unfortunate and inequitable, but it was and to some extent still is the reality. At the risk of essentializing, I will hypothesize that it may have to do, as well, with men's being more likely to work in hierarchical structures and modes, whereas women may be more likely to work in and thrive in more collegial modes. In any case, in this chapter, my topic is fathers: my own father and my academic "fathers."

My father, Dr. John Vandrick, an extraordinary man, physician, and father, died in 2003, at the age of 78, of multiple myeloma, a cancer of the blood and bone. Even as I type these lines, I find it hard to believe that he is actually gone. As Joan Didion (2005) did about her husband's death, I have engaged in a type of "magical thinking," dealing with my father's death fairly calmly, because I have secretly believed that it is just a temporary state, and that of course he will be back and everything will return to normal; it is only recently that I have more truly understood and accepted his absence, his death. I still mourn him, and I always will, but the perspective provided by the few years since his death has allowed me to appreciate him more than ever.

For years I took for granted having parents who loved me and my brothers unconditionally, who always put us first, and who always acted ethically and with kindness. I assumed all parents were like mine. Only as a young adult did I start to see and understand how unusual they were. Throughout the years, I have heard so many stories—from friends, acquaintances, and books—about terrible fathers, absent fathers, drunk fathers, distant fathers, abusive fathers, neglectful fathers, inept fathers. My students, too, often talk or write about their fathers, whom they generally admire but very often describe as stern, distant, needing to be placated, honored, obeyed. One Japanese female student, for example, wrote carefully about her father, about how he was often distant, and seldom very loving or attentive to her, her mother, or her sister; yet the student made excuses for her father, and made sure to list his good qualities: his success in business, his providing well for the family. Her story illustrates the longing that children have to focus on the positive aspects of their parents, especially fathers, because it is too painful to admit that one's father is not perfect, or might not love one absolutely.

The children of these fathers—even well into their own adulthood and often into old age—so often still adore them, need them, dream of them, even when they are justifiably angry at them. They long for their fathers' approval. Three of my friends had alcoholic fathers who died relatively young; despite acknowledging their fathers' weaknesses, these "adult children" seem to have idealized them, even to the point of choosing them over their mothers as their preferred parents. Children of difficult fathers can't stop talking about them, and if they are writers, can't stop writing about them, whether directly or in fictionalized form. Some of the most prominent fathers in literature have been some of the most problematic for their children. Think, for example, of Shakespeare's King Lear (1623/2005), or of the fathers in Arthur Miller's *Death of a Salesman* (1949/1999), Jane Smiley's *A Thousand Acres* (1991), and Edward St. Aubyn's trilogy of novels (2003). Or read Sylvia Plath's poems, especially "Daddy," in which she compares her late father to a Nazi: "the brute/Brute heart of a brute like you" (1966, p. 50).

Why did it take me so long to truly realize how fortunate I was to have a father who was present, caring, kind, ethical, and a model for how to live in the world? Why did I take this for granted? Of course (but why of course?) I always loved and appreciated him, and wanted his approval. But I was innocent and protected by his goodness and presence; the very thing that made him so wonderful a father was the thing that kept me from realizing how fortunate I was. Was this because he too had a sort of innocence about him, although he was extremely intelligent and very wise, and although he had experienced so much during his lifetime? Or was it because he himself was marked for life by his father's leaving his mother and his family of nine children when he, the youngest, was only two years old? Was that why he became a psychiatrist in midlife, after many years as a surgeon? And although he never spoke negatively to us children about his father, the grandfather whom we never knew, was his father always present to him as a negative example? As a wound, a wound he would make sure we, his children, never experienced? I never thought much about this connection, because my father never alluded to it, but was it a constant thorn, and at the same time, a constant motivation to be a good father, the good father he himself never had? Did he think about it all the time? How did he *know* how to be such a good father, with no direct model? Did he teach himself? Was it due to his mother's and sisters' loving him so much? To his own strength and perseverance over adversity, allowing him to rise from his poor (although loved and cultured) background to get an education, become a physician, be a missionary in India, have a happy 55-year marriage, and raise four mainly well-adjusted, happy, and productive children? And to make an impact on so many people's lives, including those of his many, many patients over the years? Where did that strength, that goodness, come from? Was he one of those born to it? Or was it his family? His religion? Should I have asked him more about this when he was alive? Did I not want to know about anything difficult in my father's life, preferring to believe that he was as calm and happy as he seemed to be? Would it have been too painful for me? Or was I just oblivious, as children are about their parents' lives? Even children who are now middle-aged themselves? Or was it, again, that I just took it for granted that the story had a happy ending, my father had a good adulthood, and he was a good father, so there was no need to investigate negative aspects of the past?

I am still, in my late 50s, innocent and protected in many ways. Yes, I have experienced some troubles—at work, mostly, but also in my personal life. But they have been nothing, nothing, compared to being abandoned by one's father, as my father was. I had the pure, unearned privilege of being protected by my parents' love and caring. I was just very, very lucky. I don't know the odds, but I know that the older I get, the more I learn from friends and others of all the other possibilities, all the ways that one can be denied this privilege. One friend who was less fortunate than I in her father and her family background told me once that I was the only person she knew who had a happy childhood.

I thought she was joking, or at least exaggerating, but she claimed not to be, and detailed one by one the problematic backgrounds and parents of all her other friends.

How did I not fully appreciate this great gift and great fortune? And how did I not see that this gift lasts a whole lifetime? And perhaps beyond, because I hope I have passed the gift on to my own daughter. One of this gift's legacies, among many others, is a naturally optimistic outlook on life. Although it has occasionally made me naïve and vulnerable, overall this outlook has served me well and enabled me to enjoy and savor my life; I am deeply grateful to my father (and mother too) for passing on this gift.

Besides his general influence on me, my father even influenced—and still influences—my writing. I realized this most poignantly about three years after his death, when I finally made the connection that one of the reasons I was undergoing a sort of writing block or drought was that I missed having him as a reader for my writing. I could no longer show my published work to my father, as I had been doing for so many years. All my life, I had brought my achievements, from small to large, to my parents, knowing they would lavish approval on me. It's not that I didn't feel secure of my father's love and approval no matter what (he didn't necessarily agree with all my decisions, but I knew he loved me deeply and supported me always). But I knew he would give close attention to whatever I did or wrote, and would be so proud of me. He always and immediately actually read with attention whatever I wrote for publication, and gave me feedback, always both positive and supportive. He honored my work by taking it seriously, by showing interest in it, and by understanding why it was important to me. I was so happy and proud to share my achievements—including my publications—with him.

After my father's death, I felt on some unconscious level that since I knew he wouldn't see my work published, it seemed somehow less important to keep writing. At that point in my life and publishing career, when I had already received some minor recognition, within the TESOL field, of my research and publications, I didn't really need my father's approval; another way in which he was so wonderful is that although he expected us to uphold high ethical standards, he never made us feel that he was judging us based on our grades or achievements. So I was more fortunate than, for example, the sociologist Laurel Richardson, who notes, as I do, that her "father, though long dead, was . . . still directing [her] relationship to her work," but in her case it was because he expected and assumed she would always do well in school, and gave her no recognition or praise for what was simply expected (1997, p. 24). However, although I didn't *need* my own father's approval, it was something I missed after his death, and still miss.

Another, related way in which my writing block may have been connected to my father's death is the visceral way in which a parent's death reminds us of mortality, including our own mortality. That suddenly vivid sense of impermanence may make many aspects of life seem unimportant in the larger scheme of life. Although I did not recognize this at the time, I now believe that I experienced a sense that I could labor over an article or book project for months or years, yet whatever I produced would mean very little in the face of the enormous natural forces of life and death. What was the point? Would I just be deluding myself that anyone would read my work, that it would mean anything to anyone, that it would add to the body of knowledge in our field, that anyone would care anything about it now, or ten or twenty years from now, let alone longer? I should note that this is not my usual way of thinking; as mentioned above, I am by nature an optimist and a positive thinker. Although I sometimes lack confidence about my writing, I believe strongly in the power of ideas, of words, of scholarship. But my father's death, at least for a while, changed my natural attitude and made me feel it was rather meaningless to keep writing. One of the ways I have been overcoming that feeling, once I realized it, has been to write about my father, as I am doing here.

In general, although there are of course exceptions, one's professors, bosses, and mentors cannot compare to one's own father in depth of connection and influence, but such "father figures" can be very important in one's professional life. I have had many good professors, supervisors, and senior colleagues, but three stand out; each of these three made a very real difference in my professional, and by extension personal, life.

The first of these, Professor Shigeo Imamura, was both my professor and mentor in graduate school and my supervisor at the English Language Center where I taught as a graduate student. Later, when he was asked to go as a visiting professor to set up an ESL program at a university across the country, he hired me, along with two others from my graduate program and several others from other universities, to help him set up the program and to teach at this university, the one where I have since spent my whole career. I was honored by his choosing me to work with him, and started the new job with great excitement. Unfortunately, for reasons beyond Professor Imamura's control, reasons having to do with university politics and certain administrators' personalities, the job turned out to be an extremely stressful and difficult one, both for me and for my colleagues. But Professor Imamura was always supportive, even helping me find a new position during the two years that I was temporarily laid off (along with many other faculty members at the university, including most of the ESL faculty). When he returned to his own university, we continued to keep in touch for the rest of his life, and I could always count on him for advice and encouragement.

Professor Imamura was a sort of academic father to me in that he first taught and mentored me as I started out in the field of TESOL/applied linguistics, both formally in the classroom and informally as a supervisor and colleague. He also introduced me to others in the field, encouraged me to write classroom materials and program curricula, to present papers at conferences, and to write and publish. I learned a lot from him about the field of TESOL, about pedagogy, about international students, about culture(s), and about leading one's professional and personal lives ethically and gracefully. He was always supportive of my work, and proud of my successes.

He died in 1998, and I still miss him. I keep in touch with his widow, Mrs. Isako Imamura. And at her request, two others of his former graduate students and I edited the memoir he had left behind, describing his unusual, complex bicultural and bilingual life (Imamura, 2001), a task we were honored to do in tribute to him and his influence on the field and on our careers and lives.

During the difficult time early in my career at the university (a time that I have described elsewhere, but in more general terms; see Chapters 4 and 8 for more details), another mentor, of a rather different sort, became very important to me. Professor Michael Lehmann was the founder and president of the Faculty Association at my university; this association was, among other things, a union. Professor Lehmann knew that the current situation at the university was not a just and productive one for faculty, and he, along with other dedicated colleagues, used the union to try to right those wrongs and bring more justice and equity to the university. Among other causes, he took up the cause of the ESL faculty, and fought the university administration in order to protect our jobs and our rights, and to ensure us a less abusive and more equitable workplace. The path was long, difficult, and painful, but he never faltered, never let us down. Finally, he—and we—prevailed. Our jobs were reinstated, our working conditions were made equivalent to those of other university faculty, and some protections were put into place. Financial settlements were made to those of us who had either been laid off or unjustly underpaid. Although we continued under some of the same administrators, and although there were more difficulties for some years to come, we survived and, eventually, flourished. I cannot thank Professor Lehmann enough (although I have often told him, and the other Faculty Association officials of that time period, of my deep appreciation) not only for saving our jobs and ensuring our rights, but also for their unwavering support during those long, difficult years. They also gave us a great gift: they helped us to remember that these *were* unfair working conditions we were laboring under, and that we deserved better. Sometimes when one is abused for a long time, one begins to believe that perhaps one is in fact not deserving of better treatment, or even that it is somehow one's fault for not trying harder, not doing better, in order to prevent the abuse. This is a type of thinking that will be familiar to anyone who knows anything about the experiences and thoughts of victims of domestic abuse, for example; it can and does exist in abusive workplaces as well.

The third supervisor/mentor/"academic father" that I was particularly fortunate to have was a new Dean of the College of Arts and Sciences that our program was part of. This Dean, Dr. Stanley Nel, had been, as a faculty member in the Physics Department, active in the aforementioned Faculty Association. After he became Dean, he had the power to effect change in a new and dramatic way, and he did so. He understood the needs, rights, and responsibilities of faculty, and took them seriously. He was far from uncritically supportive of all faculty or all their claims, but he was recognized as someone who was fair, and who advocated for faculty, believing that equitable treatment makes for a strong faculty, which makes for a strong college and university. In the specific case of the ESL faculty, he understood that it was grossly inequitable that we had heavier teaching loads than other faculty, were required to be physically present on campus most of the day, did not have private offices or telephones, were prevented from going to necessary meetings, were often verbally harassed and abused, and had generally been seriously mistreated. He methodically set about remedying these situations. Of course it was not easy, especially as our direct supervisor, who was a major part of the problem, was quite entrenched, and was used to being supported by the upper administration. Step by step, though, Dean Nel made the necessary changes to bring us to parity with other faculty members at the university; he also eased out our direct supervisor, who was the program administrator, and made our program a department, with an elected faculty member as chair. Dean Nel continued to be supportive of my colleagues and me for the many years he was Dean of the College, and I will always be grateful to him as well.

The USC Center for Excellence in Teaching (CET) (2003) lists mentoring roles in higher education as follows: advisor, role model, coach, and advocate. My father, most of all, was all of these to me, as were my three university "fathers"/mentors: Professor Imamura, Professor Lehmann, and Dean Nel. Some of the qualities of a good mentor listed by the USC CET (2003) are "committed to the mentoring process," "responds to individual circumstances," "encourages and motivates others," "willing to share knowledge"; my father and the three mentors also share these qualities. (For other helpful sources on mentoring, see Goodwin, Stevens, & Bellamy, 1998; Jarvis, 1991; Murray, 1991; Schoenfeld & Magnan, 1994; and my favorite resource for women in academe, Toth, 1997.)

Note that mentors, including mine, do not necessarily follow what we might think of as "classic" models. Professor Imamura, as both my professor and then my supervisor, came closest to that model. Professor Lehmann was important in my career because, as the president of the Faculty Association (union), he fought to protect the rights of the faculty, including the ESL faculty. Dean Nel was my supervisor, and his most important contribution to my career (and of course the careers of many others at USF) was to fight for equity and fairness for all faculty in his college, including the TESOL faculty. Of course the roles were blurred: Dean Nel, for example, also gave me advice about when to apply for promotion, what to do to be ready for that process, and other such more traditional academic mentoring. My point is that we should not have too narrow a concept of what mentoring is or can be. In some cases, what we need is to have advocates, and be advocates, for ourselves, our colleagues, our students, and our discipline.

Because the field of TESOL is still relatively young, and has not been a powerful field, we may have less of a tradition of mentoring than most other disciplines do; however, we may actually have more need for mentoring than some, because of the way the field and its faculty are often treated as "lesser." Thus it is important for us in TESOL to seek mentors, to mentor each other, to share knowledge and strategies, to seek allies within our institutions, and to advocate for each other.

Note that even the concept of mentoring is class-inflected. There are two general types or concepts of mentoring, in two different types of sites. The first usually involves someone of a middle (or higher) class status mentoring someone—often a child or a young person—who is in a working-class or poor family and setting. This is the Big Brothers and Big Sisters model, and it is an admirable one, one that has had some great successes. The second type is the corporate—or in our case, academic—model, in which both mentors and mentees are generally middle or upper middle class, but the mentors are further along in their careers, and assist and advise the younger mentees starting off on their career. Both of these models are valuable, although both also have some risks. In the first type, there is a danger that mentors will, perhaps unwittingly, see themselves as generous rescuers helping poor children and young people; the mentees may also see the mentors as condescending, or as lacking understanding of their situations. There may be communication problems arising from class differences. In the second case, in which mentors and mentees are mostly from the same social class background, class is much less an issue, but there may be complications arising from gender or other identities. When the mentors are men and the mentees are women, sexist power relationships may be reinforced, with men in a position of power over women. There may also be sexual tensions, or even sexual exploitation of the mentoring relationship. Although I was very fortunate in the mentors I describe in this chapter, and write about them to celebrate these dedicated individuals who helped me so much, I do mourn the fact that I, and most other women early in their careers, did not have more female mentors.

My stories in this chapter, like the other stories in this volume, illustrate ways in which the possession or lack of possession of privilege pervades every aspect of our lives. This is as true in academe as elsewhere. In my own case, areas in which I lacked privilege within the university, especially in the early years, were being in ESL, a field that is still relatively new and that lacks status; being female; being very young; and being non-religious at a religion-based university. It is particularly difficult and even galling to notice that many in academe do not understand the field of TESOL, do not accord it recognition as a legitimate discipline and field of research, and often condescend to those of us in the field. However, I must also acknowledge the areas of privilege that helped me even at the most difficult times at my university: being white, middle-class, heterosexual; having a full-time job; and, eventually, having the help and support of some powerful men within the university, as I have described in this chapter. Although I suffered (and sometimes still suffer) because of the areas in which I lacked privilege, I was able to survive and prosper at least in part because of the areas in which I did have privilege, along with a bit of luck; even "luck" seems to come more often to those who already have privilege as a foundation, and who have the resources, the social capital, to take advantage of the "luck" when it comes along. Although I was fortunate to have these areas of privilege, I fully acknowledge that some of these (most obviously race, social class, sexual identity) are areas of unearned privilege, areas in which we in academe must work for more equity.

Circling back to the beginning of this chapter, I can see how in addition to the privilege that has directly affected me and my career, as outlined here, I also had the even deeper foundation of privilege provided by having loving, middle-class parents, who were able to support me both emotionally (by believing in me, shoring me up) and, when necessary, financially, providing me with the luxury of a safety net. This privilege was then reinforced by my good fortune in having the support of my academic "fathers"/mentors, who also believed in me, and more importantly, believed in equity and justice.

I give much credit to my university, and to many other universities, for vastly improving recruitment, working conditions, support, and retention of women and minorities as faculty members in recent years. In specific regarding the "stepchild" field of TESOL, I give my university much credit for recognizing our field as worthy of equal treatment within academe. However, throughout academe there is still much to be done regarding equity for women, minorities, and less-established academic fields. We may never be able to erase all inequities and injustices in academe, but we can certainly do much more. Although much of what needs to be done can only be done at societal and institutional levels, we as individuals can also press for change. We, female and male, can also be mentors, sharing our own knowledge and support with colleagues, and using any positions of responsibility that we attain for the good of others in our field. This is, to me, one of the biggest tasks we in TESOL need to work on during the years ahead.

Chapter 6

Gender, Class, and
the Balanced Life

Valerie, a Korean woman in her late 20s, is an extremely bright, mature, and ambitious student in my Advanced ESL Reading/Writing class. She is interesting, interested, focused, a class leader, and a joy to have in class. She speaks to me in my office one day, telling me how determined she is that nothing will stop her from attaining her goal of a graduate degree in theater management, and a career in that field. She tells me that she made sure her husband was comfortable with her goals before she agreed to marry him.

A little over a year later, now both a graduate student and a mother, Valerie dashes to her first class in the program she has just entered, worrying about her English ability in this class full of native speakers, and simultaneously worrying about leaving her new baby for too long. At the class break, she dashes out to her car, where her husband is waiting with the baby, and hurriedly breastfeeds him, then dashes back to class again, still worrying about both class and baby. She is fast learning about the juggling act that many women with her goals encounter.

Valerie's story illustrates a situation many women with careers, or aspirations for careers, encounter. When I became involved with the women's movement almost 40 years ago, I optimistically thought that barriers to women's equity and opportunity would soon fall. I, like many, underestimated the deep (and not always conscious) roots of society's bias against such equality. Even young women such as Valerie who are privileged as far as social class status often find it difficult to succeed in their careers, especially if they are balancing those careers with having children.

For many years now, I have been very interested in gender issues, in general, and in specific in pedagogy, and from an even more specific perspective, in ESOL pedagogy. On the personal and political level, I have studied, read about, thought about, written about, and been involved in women's issues and feminism since the late 1960s, when the "women's liberation" movement, later known as second wave feminism, began. I well remember my "consciousness raising group" of the early 1970s, and I still have on my bookshelf badly copied pamphlets with titles such as "The Myth of Women's Inferiority" (Reed, n.d.), "Sex Roles and Female Oppression" (Densmore, n.d.), and "Female Liberation as the Basis for Social Revolution" (Dunbar, n.d.). Throughout my teaching career, I have always taught about, and my teaching has always been informed by, social and political issues, and in particular gender issues. I recently ran across an audiotape of myself giving a lecture to the gathered students of our ESL program in about 1977; as I listened to the tape after so many years, I was struck by how strongly I felt at the time, and began musing about how much has changed and how much has remained the same during the more than 30 years since then. I know that many advances have been made by women, in civil rights, in careers, in medical care, in religious arenas, in sports, and more, and I am very happy to have been part of this era of advancement. However, I am daily reminded of the widespread discrimination and inequity that still exist for women.

I am not sure why I was so early and so strongly drawn to feminism and women's issues. One possible answer is that I come from a family of strong women: my mother, grandmothers, and aunts. In addition, the men in my family—especially my father and brothers—have always believed in the equality of women, and have had very egalitarian marriages. Also, my parents raised me with a strong sense of the importance of equity and justice for all. So when the late sixties/early seventies iteration of the women's movement came along during my teenage and college years, it felt very right and natural to become part of it. Gender issues, women's issues, women's lives, women's literature, and women's stories have been a major focus of my life and work ever since.

As for my scholarly work, many of my publications (e.g., Vandrick, 1994a, 1995b, 1998, 1999a, 1999c, 2004) have been about gender and pedagogy. Although others in our field (e.g., Davis & Skilton-Sylvester, 2004; Kubota, 2003; Norton, 2000; Norton & Pavlenko, 2004; Pavlenko, Blackledge, Piller, & Teutsch-Dwyer, 2001; Schenke, 1991, 1996) have given attention to this topic and made important and useful contributions to our knowledge in this area, I am concerned that the subject is still not a priority in TESOL.

I have also been interested in issues of social class and ways in which they play out in ESOL settings; in particular, I have explored issues related to class privilege. Further, I have begun to explore intersections of gender and class/privilege in ESOL. In this chapter I look at how educated female international students with professional experience or aspirations are affected by these intersections and ways in which the intersections play out in students' lives. This question has resonance for me, as it does for most female academics, as I too have lived out some of the struggles regarding being a woman academic, and I have seen the different ways in which both gender and class, and their intersections, affect women trying to succeed in academe, especially women who also have children or want to do so. I also think about how the options for women have in some ways changed greatly, but in other ways have not changed nearly enough, in the years since I was starting off as a graduate student, continuing in my career, and balancing my career with my family. I think with both pride and trepidation about my mid-20s aged daughter and her generation as they start out on their careers. To illustrate some aspects of these gender- and class-related questions, particularly as they apply to international women graduate students, I will focus, later in this chapter, on the example of Valerie, the former student with whom I had many discussions about her life, her dilemmas, and her decision-making processes.

Although it is useful to look at intersections of gender and class, it is important not to look at them as parallel. For one thing, people sometimes can and do change their social class status during their lives; they much more rarely change their gender identity. I, as a middle-class woman, would not presume to say that gender is more limiting than class, since as a middle-class professional person, I have seldom experienced being negatively limited by class. However, I would like to explore in this chapter ways in which gender is, at least for middle and upper class women, still—despite their class privilege—a limiting factor in their lives.

When speaking of class, it is perhaps hard for many people to devote much attention or sympathy to the problems of the affluent and privileged, or even of the middle class. I understand this, but I believe that as educators, we need to look at the whole spectrum of backgrounds from which our students come, including those at the higher end of the class spectrum, and to try to understand their situations and their concerns.

Social class affects every aspect of our lives, and it is a major factor that intersects with gender. Consider, for example, the complex dynamics of the current condition of women in the workplace. Many women in the United States of the middle and upper classes now have enormous opportunities as far as education and careers, opportunities that were almost unheard of as recently as 30 years ago. In 1971 (just before Title IX was passed), less than 10 percent of students in medical schools were female; in 2005, women formed nearly 50 percent of medical school students. During the same time period, female law school students increased from about 7 percent to nearly 49 percent (Musil, 2007, p. 43). Women have had unprecedented success in politics, business, law, post-secondary education, and the arts.

However, there are some huge caveats to these success stories. First, there are still glass ceilings in many professions. Second, it continues to be difficult for women to balance professional and other high-level careers with motherhood; as Linda Hirshman puts it, "The glass ceiling begins at home" (Walsh, 2006, n.p.). The percentage of adult women working outside the home has stalled since 1995, and even recently slipped from a high of 77 percent in 2000 to 75 percent in 2005 (Porter, 2006). Why has this happened? Society has been slow to provide the kinds of laws and support systems needed for such balance. Fathers do more childcare than in the past, but the main weight of childcare is still borne by mothers. The model for success in high-powered careers is still the male model of the past: one must show one's dedication by putting in long hours and intense work, especially in the early years when one is proving oneself in order to get tenure at a university, or be promoted to partner in a law firm, or be considered for vice president of a bank or corporation. My daughter is now in law school, and I am concerned about her facing this dilemma, especially if she works for one of the large law firms that routinely require their young lawyers to work 80 hours a week. When she worked at such a firm as a paralegal before beginning law school, she noted that the women who reached the partner level there were mostly unmarried and all childless. Will she be able to have the family she wants and still aspire to the highest levels in her chosen field? What sacrifices will she have to make, sacrifices that a young man in the same situation would not have to make, at least to the same extent?

So, paradoxically, the women who have the social capital and the education to reach the high positions that we feminists fought for (among other goals) are still forced either to renounce motherhood, or to try desperately to balance their careers and their parenting, always feeling they are shortchanging one or the other or both.

I do not mean to ignore or minimize the balancing act that women of the working class and/or of poverty have to manage. Although the jobs they do may not require the same level of education as the professional positions of educated women, they are in some ways harder jobs, more wearing physically and mentally; in addition, such women have far less financial and social capital, far fewer resources to cushion the problems that arise. But in this chapter, in order to examine a specific dimension of the social class and gender axis, I focus on the irony that the women who have the most class resources are still limited because of gender.

First let's look, for a moment, at the numerous news stories about women with Ivy League educations and advanced professional degrees who, once they have children, are choosing to quit their jobs and stay home, some temporarily but many permanently. A *Time* magazine story (Wallis, 2004) stated that 22 percent of U.S. mothers with professional and graduate degrees are staying home with their children (p. 53). Recent stories in the *New York Times* (Belkin, 2003) and on the television news program *60 Minutes* (Staying at home, 2005), among other media outlets, assert that the most elite of these educated and privileged women are even more likely to give up their careers and stay home once they have children. For example, in 2000, only 38 percent of women with Harvard MBAs were working full time (Belkin, 2003).

These articles are somewhat sensationalistic, and may reflect the lives of only a fraction of successful women; further, the articles lack any critical analysis of societal reasons for women deciding to stay home. The stories certainly lack any critical stance on the social class aspects of the reported phenomenon. Perhaps too, the media are all too eager to find examples of the supposed "failures" of feminism. But the fact remains that some very educated and privileged women are deciding to stay home. Rather than look at this as an individual decision, or as a sign of the failure of feminism, some have noted that—as one article (Porter, 2006) put it—mothers had since the 1960s

> rejiggered bits of their lives, extracting more time
> to accommodate jobs and careers from every
> nook and cranny of the day. They married later
> and had fewer children. They turned to laborsaving
> machines and paid others to help handle household
> work; they persuaded the men in their lives to do
> more chores. (p. A2)

But now those women are finding that there is no more time to squeeze out—they have "hit a wall in the amount of work they can pack into a week" (p. A2).

These same dilemmas affect, or will affect, students in our ESOL classes. Over years of teaching, I have often noted that young female international students in my classes expressed the kinds of lack of confidence in themselves that Hancock (1989), Pipher (1995), and others have written about among young women in the United States. One of my students, for example, wrote, "I don't think that I am a good leader. I have always learned how to obey or follow what my parents said, my older brothers said, my teachers said. I almost forgot how to think by myself." Two other young women in my classes wrote, completely independently of each other, in different years, that they had been active girls, classic tomboys, and that their mothers had always told them not to be like that; in both cases, they eventually fell (I cannot help noticing the symbolism of "falling" from grace, Eve-like), one from a tree and one from a wall, and were told that the falls were punishment for acting in unfeminine ways. Both girls, sadly, felt that their mothers' views had been vindicated, and both girls determined to be less active and more careful from then on.

However, I have also noted and described ways in which for some socially privileged international/ESL students, including privileged women students, social class "trumped" gender (and other identities) as most important and influential in their lives, alleviating some of the disadvantages of being female (and/or of having other less privileged identities) (e.g., Vandrick, 1995a, 2007, in press). I have seen in my classes and in other interactions with my students that some of my (mainly Asian) undergraduate international women students—like my undergraduate American students and like many American high school girls (see Kindlon, 2006, on "alpha girls")—feel very comfortable with their privileged positions and their social capital, and do not think that they will have problems being successful in their careers and blending their careers with marriage and motherhood. They are used to being well supported in every way, and expect that their lives will continue on the same path of privilege; they do not see gender as a serious obstacle. I worry about these students because of their lack of awareness of all the gender issues and problems that still remain for women, and I am sorry that their class privilege often prevents them from being sensitive to the situations of those with less privilege.

In contrast, in recent years I have had many more graduate, pre-professional, or professional women students in my classes, and I have found a distinct difference in their attitudes and expectations, in contrast with the undergraduates described above. These students, being a bit older and a bit closer to their post-education adult lives, have started to be aware that despite their social class privilege and their former confident sense that they can do anything, they will probably encounter difficulties and limitations as they make decisions about careers, marriage, and family. In particular, once they have children, gender again becomes the dominant identity, and class privilege, although it definitely still alleviates some of the inequities experienced by women, provides less protection than it did before they had children.

Because it is illustrative, and because I believe in the power of stories, let me now tell you (with her permission) the story of one woman

ESOL student who faced this dilemma, the one I alluded to earlier in this chapter, and who featured in the two vignettes that begin this chapter. Valerie (she uses an English name, although not this one), a Korean student in her late 20s, after graduating from college worked in theater management for several years. At the same time as she was starting her career, she married a fellow Korean she had known for three years. She told me that her husband knew that it was her dream to have a career in theater, and that he supported that dream; she would not have married him if he had not. However, when she interviewed for jobs in Korea after she got married, many companies asked if she was married, if she planned to have children, and whether she would quit work if she had children; she felt sure that she was rejected for some jobs because she was a married woman. She also pointed out that it was hard for women in Korea who had quit work to stay home with young children to then re-enter the workforce.

Valerie and her husband came to the United States to study, she to get a master's degree in theater management, and he to earn a master's degree in film production. At the time I first met Valerie, her husband had just started his master's studies, and she was studying ESL and applying to master's programs. The twist was that she had recently become pregnant. Although it was an unplanned pregnancy, she and her husband were becoming excited about the idea of becoming parents. However, Valerie was also extremely concerned that motherhood would delay her studies and her career.

For context, let's look at Valerie's background. Her parents and her parents-in-law were upper middle class; all four had at least bachelor's degrees and the two fathers had master's degrees. Valerie's mother worked in a business, as did her mother-in-law until she retired early. Valerie's mother had been a professional-level pianist until she married just out of college and stopped performing; she felt that she had given up her dream, and thus told Valerie from the time she was a young girl that for girls it was extremely important that they got an education, followed their dreams, and had fulfilling careers. At the same time, Valerie received mixed messages, because after her marriage, the parents on both sides constantly asked when she was going to have children, and thought it was very strange and wrong that after seven years of marriage, and in her late 20s, she had no children. The parents were ecstatic about the new grandchild, and doted on him.

Valerie wanted to continue her studies immediately after her child was born, but was persuaded by her parents to stay home with him for a semester. She then, as described in the second vignette at the beginning of this chapter, began attending class again and taking care of her child. Valerie's parents, who lived in the United States but in another city, offered to take care of her child, and she considered but rejected that option. It was an option that would have helped her focus on her studies and finish sooner, but it would mean that she and her husband would have only seen their child on weekends and vacations. (This arrangement is more common and more culturally acceptable in Korea and some other countries than it might be in the United States.) Valerie loved her son, but was conflicted about the constraints that motherhood put on her life and her ambitions. She told me that her friends who have had babies suddenly changed completely, and gave up all their plans regarding studies and work; she didn't seem to feel this could happen to her, but the possibility lingered in the back of her mind and concerned her deeply.

For further context regarding Valerie's story: She told me that all her high school friends went to women's colleges, graduated, married, maybe worked for a short while in fairly low-level jobs such as "office girl," and then had children and quit work. Her college friends, on the other hand, were working on graduate degrees and were determined not to marry or have children, or at least not until they had finished their doctoral or other advanced degrees and become established in their careers, or maybe never. Valerie closely observed the two very divergent approaches, and found neither of them acceptable for herself, yet of course had concerns about how she could pursue and maintain her dream career and also be a mother. She was buffeted by Korean society's prescriptions, by her parents' and parents-in-laws' expectations, by her friends' various and conflicting experiences, and by her own ambivalence and fear.

Valerie had a difficult time during the semester she took time off from classes; although she dearly loved her baby, she felt isolated staying home with him, and worried that she was getting behind in her English ability and in her education and career. Once she started taking classes again, although it was hard, she felt much happier. Her life did get easier with time, and I was happy to see her taking pleasure in her role as mother, and simultaneously gaining confidence as a student contributing to class discussions and writing papers in English in her graduate classes. Like many mothers of young children, she will continue to struggle with balancing these two aspects of her life.

What interests—and frankly, saddens—me about Valerie's story, and the stories of other young women like her, is this: American women (along with women from some other countries) began this wave of "liberation" and access to better opportunity, education, and careers, and these opportunities were especially available to those with class privilege, yet they have hit a new kind of glass ceiling because of the age-old dilemma of balancing a successful career and a family. Even class privilege does not exempt women from this dilemma. Young women from Korea and other Asian countries have come a little later to educational and career opportunities, and society's support for such opportunities, but they are now bumping up against the same dilemmas regarding career and family. Again, class privilege does not exempt them. Although class privilege provides so many advantages, so much social capital, to upper-class and upper middle-class women, and although in some ways class does outweigh gender in its influence (preventing, for example, the ills of poverty), it apparently cannot and does not alleviate the lack of societal will to make the kinds of fundamental changes that would allow women to combine successful careers and motherhood.

Of course all societies should provide such support to all women at all social levels. My point here is that as important as social class is in determining the direction of people's lives, and although social class often "trumps" gender, in the case of privileged women, gender can still negate or lessen some class advantages. Gender is still a powerful locus of oppression at all levels of almost all societies.

Most societies have not evolved enough on this issue. It is true that some European and other countries are much further along than the majority of countries in supporting working women and families. But in most countries, including the United States, figuring out how to balance career and family is still considered an individual problem, rather than a societal issue and responsibility. Thus women of class privilege, because they have the advantage of more resources, and because they are so busy and perhaps blind to their own privilege, manage to patch together the best solutions they can for themselves, and don't usually work on broader societal solutions that would benefit all women. So unfortunately the very women who have the most privilege, and therefore should take the most responsibility to change society, use their own privilege either to opt out of the whole dilemma, or to cobble together their own individual solutions. This to me is one of the most unfortunate problems about class differences: they divide groups that need to stick together and work for the common good, such as women; in other words, class can and often does get in the way of women's solidarity and progress. And, as Valerie's story illustrates, both gender and social class also seem to outweigh culture as a defining characteristic, at least in this arena: Women of different cultures experience the same problems when they make decisions about their lives, and women of different social classes have different resources for dealing with the problems, but none escapes the problems completely.

So I, along with other instructors of international women students, am left to worry about the future lives of these students, and to wonder how I can best assist them, as their teacher and advisor. What do I tell the Valeries in my classes? How do I respond when they write in their journals about these dilemmas and fears, and when they come to me for advice? On the one hand, I want to praise them for furthering their educations and for having career goals, and I want to encourage them; on the other hand, I want to be realistic with them about what might lie ahead. I, like many other educators, have experienced the same dilemmas in my own life, and I can and do sometimes share with them my own stories and some of my own solutions, but each woman has to go through the struggles herself. I wish that there were more organized, formal discussion of these issues in the academic world, and in particular in TESOL. Our sister field, Composition, has done a bit more, although still not much. One book in that field is *Women's Ways of Making It in Rhetoric and Composition* (Balif, Davis, & Mountford, 2008), which sheds some useful light on the work-life balance dilemma, and addresses the problem at various stages of women academics' careers. Another recent, relevant, and useful book is *Mama PhD: Women Write about Motherhood and Academic Life* (Evans & Grant, 2008); the stories it collects are both sobering and inspiring. We need more such examinations and more such discussion in TESOL settings as well.

The world is run, unfortunately, by those with resources and privilege, generally to the detriment of those without those resources and privilege. As educators, ESL or otherwise, we have the opportunity to reach all of our students, female and male, including students of affluence who may be powerful in the future. By providing these students with knowledge about class and gender, by engaging them in critical analysis and discussion, and by supporting their exploration of these issues, we have a chance to influence them, and hope that they in turn—as they get older and perhaps wield power in their various spheres—will use their knowledge and influence in ways that will benefit all women, all families, whether or not they come from privileged backgrounds.

As I come to the end of this chapter, and as I think over my conversations with Valerie about her experiences, I realize again that her stories strike a deep chord with me, personally as well as professionally. My belief in feminism is an ever-present bedrock value in my life. I am still, after all these years, intensely concerned (dare I say angry?) about the inequities that women still suffer. Although social class—for some fortunate women—clearly mitigates some of the inequalities imposed by gender, there is still a deep divide between what is possible for women and what is possible for men. I strongly disagree with talk of "postfeminism," especially when it is intimated that sexism has been solved, and feminism is outdated. Then I give myself a talk about how much things *have* changed, and how fortunate I am to be living in an era, and in a location, where (at least some) women have infinitely more opportunity than in other eras and in other places. I remind myself that I should be grateful for the advances that have taken place. I lecture myself that I need to channel my anger about what hasn't changed into my work, my teaching, my writing. This self-talk helps, but not enough.

Chapter 7

Sexual Identity and Education

*I*t is the early 1990s. In class one day, the subject of homosexuality arises. *Immediately a nervous silence descends on the classroom. Then a male student laughs and mockingly displays an exaggerated limp wrist. Several students giggle, then stop. Everyone looks at me to see how I will handle the situation. I take a deep but shaky breath and haltingly speak to them about how prejudice or discrimination against LGBT (lesbian, gay, bisexual, and transgender) people is unfair; I tell them that the research shows that sexual identity is largely innate, biological, rather than chosen. They tell me that they don't know any gay people; I reply that they probably do, but unfortunately many LGBT people do not feel free to reveal their sexual identity, because of society's norms. Some tell me that there are no gay people in their countries. I respectfully disagree. Some tell me that homosexuality is against their religion. I say that I respect each religion's beliefs, but that I believe that LGBT rights are human rights. I have to and want to say these things, but I feel awkward and anxious, wondering how they will be received. The students seem interested but uncomfortable and embarrassed, and seem relieved when we go back to the "regular" classroom topics and activities.*

I attend an LGBT caucus meeting at a TESOL conference in the late 1990s. People are sharing their stories. A high school teacher from a rather conservative state quietly, emotionally, tells the group that he has been in a relationship for almost twenty years, yet has never once been able to mention his partner at the school where he works. As he tells his story, the room is absolutely silent, completely focused on this teacher's experience. Afterward, there are expressions of support, and more than a few tears in people's eyes. For some reason, although I have long known of such difficulties for LGBT teachers, this story hits me in a particularly visceral way, and I have never forgotten it.

I believe that we all need to be aware, in TESOL settings as well as in our larger worlds, of our own areas of privilege as well as areas in which we are less privileged. For example, I carry privilege as a white, middle-class, able-bodied heterosexual, but lack privilege in the areas of gender. I have privilege as a tenured full professor, but lack privilege as a member of a non-prestigious discipline, TESOL. In this chapter, I focus on sexual identity and its connections with privilege and lack thereof. As a heterosexual, I have much unearned privilege; my life is easier because I am part of the majority, the "norm." As in the case of other types of privilege, such as white privilege, heterosexuals often underestimate the advantages, from the significant to the everyday and trivial, that LGBTs experience. There are so many ways in which one's life is much easier because of being part of the dominant sexual identity or race. I am reminded of Peggy McIntosh's famous (1988) essay on the invisible "backpack" of privilege that white people unconsciously carry with them everywhere; there is clearly a similar set of invisible privileges that heterosexual people carry as well. For just a few examples, in addition to the many legal and civil rights they take for granted, heterosexuals can speak openly about their relationships, show pictures of their partners, and bring their partners to social functions related to work; LGBT people often cannot do these things, or do them at their own risk. Or if they do these things, they are often accused of flaunting their sexuality, something that would never be said about a straight person displaying photographs of his or her spouse and children in his office. Heteronormativity means that straight people never have to explain their sexuality or their personal relationships in a way that LGBTs have to choose, over and over again throughout their lives, to do or not to do.

Part of my focus in this book of looking at TESOL educators as "whole persons" is looking not only at our own identities, but those of our students, colleagues, and others in our institutions and organizations. The critical questions are not just which sexual identities each of those people has, but also the ways in which each of us understands and approaches issues of sexual identity, and understands and approaches those around us with various sexual identities and orientations. I believe that we in TESOL need to have more conversations about this topic.

Because of my belief in the power of personal narrative to exemplify ideas, here I write about my own "journey" throughout the years to better understanding of sexual identity, and to advocacy—especially in my ESL classes, in TESOL-related publications, and at TESOL-related conferences—for equity and justice for LGBT students and faculty. In the course of telling my story, I hope to illustrate, in particular, the following three themes. First, sexual identity is one of many identities an individual has, and always interacts with her/his other identities. Sometimes these other identities exacerbate prejudice experienced by an LGBT person; in other cases, a person's privilege in other areas ameliorates such prejudice. Second, those with privilege in one area should use that privilege to advocate for those without privilege in that area; here, I specifically suggest that heterosexuals, especially heterosexual educators, have a responsibility to advocate for justice for LGBT people, just as I believe that men should advocate for women's rights. Third, people who advocate for those with an identity different from their own need to first educate themselves on the issues, be aware of possible pitfalls in "speaking for" or representing those with different identities, and learn how to avoid these pitfalls; this is a concern that I continually struggle with. In our capacities as TESOL professionals, we have exceptional opportunities to educate on various aspects of privilege, as well as the responsibility to do so carefully and with adequate knowledge and preparation.

Of course each person's experiences are unique, but some elements of my story may resonate for some other academics. More than the specifics of my story, what I hope to demonstrate is the complicated ways in which our own experiences shape our perceptions of, and responses to, others with various identities. In addition, I hope to make the point that although we are shaped by our experiences, we are also able to transcend the effects of those experiences, if we determine that we need to do so in order to work for equity and justice for all people, regardless of their identities.

In this chapter on sexual identity, I focus on the above themes in the contexts of TESOL and second language education, of the experiences of LGBT students and faculty in second language education settings, and of ways in which LGBT/queer issues are addressed in those settings, but I hope that my experiences and thoughts will connect with those of other educators and students as well.

Let me pause here for a brief discussion of the terminology I use in this chapter. I use the term *sexual identity*, as many scholars do, to encompass what are in fact two different concepts. The first is actual gender identity, which includes—at minimum—the categories male, female, transgender, and intersex; in certain cultural contexts, there have been "Third" and "Fourth" genders, including the Native American *berdache* and two-spirit, and the South Asian *hijra*. The second, more common use of the term refers to one's sexual orientation, in other words to whom one is attracted sexually; here the most common categories are heterosexual, homosexual (lesbian and gay), bisexual, and questioning. I also use the term *LGBT* (lesbian, gay, bisexual, and transgender) to refer to people with these minority sexualities. I occasionally use the word *homosexual,* but prefer not to use it regularly, as some scholars believe that "the word homosexual has a medical connotation that conjures up all the wrong imagery" (Tierney, 1997, p. 11). Many theorists and activists now use the formerly denigrating but now reclaimed term *queer* to cover all of these categories and more, in order to indicate the multiple and fluid nature of sexuality and sexual orientation. I occasionally use this term as well, particularly in the context of "queer theory," upon which I draw to some extent in this chapter.

Queer theory asserts that sexuality is fluid, and does not privilege any variety of sexuality over others; it rejects the use of the term *normal,* believing that the term privileges heterosexuality. Britzman (1995) gives us a brief description of queer theory, stating that it is "an attempt to move away from psychological explanations like homophobia, which individualizes heterosexual fear and/or loathing toward gay and lesbian subjects at the expense of examining how heterosexuality becomes normalized as natural" (p. 153). TESOL theorist Nelson (1999) prefers "queer theory" to a lesbian and gay theoretical framework because "it shifts the focus from inclusion to inquiry, that is, from including minority sexual identities to examining how language and culture work with regard to all sexual identities" (p. 371).

My Personal Journey to Understanding

As I look back and try to trace the "journey" of my interest in sexual identity issues, I realize how innocent (ignorant?) I was about such issues until my college years in the late 1960s and early 1970s. Although I knew of the existence of lesbians and gay men, I don't remember personally knowing any LGBT people, or thinking about LGBT issues, until then. Remembering my college years and after, several incidents come to mind. As with "women's liberation" during the same time period, there were the beginnings of the "gay liberation" movement on campuses. I recall the first time I saw an on-campus gathering in support of gay rights, and I vividly remember my surprise and fascination at witnessing the event. About the same time, I briefly dated a fellow student whom I will call Jeremy, wondered why he had stopped calling, and soon after saw him with a male student in a clearly romantic relationship. We spoke in a friendly way, but I will never know if during the time we dated, he hadn't yet realized he was gay, or if he was bisexual, or if he was trying to fight against his sexual identity. A few years later, when I moved to San Francisco, I began seeing and meeting many lesbians and gay men at work, at social events, on the street, and elsewhere. Eventually I also knew a few transgendered people. Identities and behaviors (e.g., men holding hands on the street, the Gay Pride parade) that had seemed exotic and unusual soon became very usual and ordinary to me.

With time, both through people I knew and through my own reading, I learned more about such topics as transgender, intersex, people whose sexual identity is fluid and who cross sexual identity lines, and political aspects of sexual identity.

As I raised my daughter in San Francisco, I was glad to see how natural it was for her to have friends with lesbian and gay parents, and as she got older, to have her own lesbian and gay friends. When she went to college in a less progressive part of the country, she was surprised to find that some of her classmates said things like, "I don't know any gay people." This atmosphere motivated her to become something of an advocate at her university for equity for LGBT people. Later, a friend's daughter, whom I had known since she was a toddler, came out as a lesbian; I recently had the pleasure of seeing an album of photos of her commitment ceremony with her partner.

In my family, professional, and city circles, there have been many occasions for celebration of progress. I was proud of the branch of my family that has a large extended family reunion every three years, and at those reunions has warmly welcomed gay family members and their partners, as well as the transgendered friend of one cousin. I was also proud of my university when it was—after much discussion and negotiation over several years—the first Jesuit university in the United States to provide benefits for "legally domiciled adults" (including domestic partners). I also celebrated and was proud of my city when its mayor, Gavin

Newsom, announced in 2004 that San Francisco would issue licenses for and perform same-sex marriages, although such marriages were not legal statewide. The action was an important one in acknowledging the unfairness of U.S. marriage laws, and in acknowledging the loving, loyal partnerships of so many lesbians and gay men. It was also important symbolically, and a step forward in the fight for civil rights for all citizens.

So, fortunately, we can see increasing evidence of numerous advances in the visibility and acceptance of lesbians and gay men; we see this progress in the passing of same-sex marriage and domestic partner laws in some states, in laws against hate crimes based on sexual identity, and in programs in schools and universities. But there are still so many problems in this area, and so much that has to be done to rectify injustices and to prevent tragedies, both in the United States setting where I live and teach, and in other countries where EFL instructors teach, and where our students come from. The legal system in the United States, for example, still does not provide equity to LGBT citizens. There is discrimination, overt and covert, in the workplace and elsewhere. Young LGBTs are still too often bullied, harassed, and even murdered. Hearing these stories showed me that there is still much work to be done, and made me feel responsible for doing what I could in this regard.

This sense of responsibility was intensified as I became more aware of LGBT students in my own and other classes. Although only a few students spoke openly of their LGBT identities, others made oblique references to them in their writing, especially in journals, which are confidential and not seen by anyone else but the instructor. Some students said nothing of their identities, but displayed alternative styles of dress or other signs. Once there was a student in my class whose gender I was unable to ascertain for the first few weeks of the semester. Another student, a young Asian woman, gradually throughout the course of the semester dressed and behaved first in an increasingly androgynous and then in an overtly masculine style, ending the semester as a seemingly

very different person with very different gender and sexual identities.
Neither of these two students confided in me, but I hope that the discussions on LGBT issues we had, and the atmosphere of acceptance and
respect that I tried to create in the classroom, provided them some support. Students such as these reminded me that LGBT students are sitting
in our ESL classes as much as anywhere else, and that their instructors
and institutions need to be aware of this.

My Academic Journey to Education and Advocacy

In the course of the life experiences I have briefly summarized above,
I became more and more concerned about the unfairness of prejudice
and discrimination against LGBTs; I saw this as a human rights issue.
Just as I had addressed issues of race and ethnicity, and especially issues
of gender, in my teaching and writing, I decided to make sure to address
sexual identity issues and LGBT rights at least briefly, in an appropriate
way, in my classes and in my scholarship and writing. As a feminist, I had
been interested in and concerned about gender issues, especially in the
form of feminist pedagogy, for a long time, and I had published several
articles and chapters related to gender. But it was becoming clear to me
that it was important not only to address issues of groups that I belong to
(in this case, women), but also to discuss issues relating to, and to advocate for, people with other identities, especially oppressed or stigmatized
identities. One reason that I believe in this responsibility is a general
belief in, and commitment to working for, fairness and equity. Another
is that sometimes it is easier for someone who is not in a certain group
to speak about and advocate for those in that group. For example, lesbian or gay ESOL teachers may be afraid that if they speak up on LGBT
issues, they will be the victims of backlash, job loss, or other forms of
harm, whereas heterosexual teachers are far less likely to have these concerns. A third reason is that we are all—all human beings—in this life
together, and what harms one group harms us all. I am reminded of
the often-cited, many-versioned poem, attributed to Martin Niemoller,

about Germany during Hitler's reign. In one version, translated from German to English (Littell, 1997), the poem states that

> First they came for the communists, and I did not speak out—
>> because I was not a communist;
> Then they came for the socialists, and I did not speak out—
>> because I was not a socialist;
> Then they came for the trade unionists, and I did not speak out—
>> because I was not a trade unionist;
> Then they came for the Jews, and I did not speak out—
>> because I was not a Jew;
> Then they came for me—
>> and there was no one left to speak out for me.

For all of these reasons, my personal journey regarding sexual identity issues has led to my academic journey on the same issues, in which I have increasingly read about, taught about, spoken about, and written about the topic.

In my teaching, I have tried to incorporate attention to LGBT issues in my classes. Some scholars/teachers have labeled such attention "queer pedagogy," a pedagogy that "worries about and unsettles normalcy's immanent exclusions" (Britzman, 1998, p. 50). There are (at least) two aspects to such attention. The first is being aware that there may be queer students in one's classroom, and being sensitive to that fact by monitoring materials, activities, and classroom discourse. Creating an accepting atmosphere for all is important not only for queer students, but for modeling and promoting accepting and respectful attitudes among heterosexual students as well. The second aspect involves specifically addressing LGBT issues in class, through one's materials and lesson plans, as well as through taking advantage of opportunities that arise naturally in classroom discussion to educate students about sexual identity issues. Moita-Lopes (2006) argues that "there is a need for openly incorporating gay and lesbian themes into classroom discourses and for queering literacy teaching" (p. 31). Sometimes this can be done by introducing sexual identity issues in the context of other identity issues, and of social justice issues (Vandrick, 1997e, 2001b). Curran (2006) argues, however, that we cannot uncritically list sexual identity issues along with other social justice issues, and that queer pedagogy "makes use of queer theory to challenge conventional understanding and practices with regard to teaching about diversity or social justice" (p. 85). Pennycook (2001), too, cautions against addressing sexual identity issues in classes as part of a laundry list of social "issues" such as the environment; he also points out that teachers must understand that "to develop antihomophobic or antiracist education requires much more than simply some rational, intellectual explanation of what's wrong with racism and homophobia. Rather we need an engagement with . . . people's investments and desires" (p. 159).

In addition to including LGBT topics in my classes, I have addressed these topics in my scholarly work. I have spoken on and written about sexual identity issues at professional conferences and in journals and other professional publications. Before I describe my own work, I would like to acknowledge the few brave pioneers who were the first to write about sexual identity in our field and related fields. They have done so despite the possibility of harming their careers; Cynthia Nelson has pointed out that one challenge of writing about sexual identity issues is "the possible professional consequences of undertaking research in an often stigmatised area" (2006b, p. 4). Yet Nelson herself is the scholar who has most prominently and consistently been a leader in research, speaking and writing about LGBT issues in TESOL/second language education. She makes a strong and convincing argument for inclusion of LGBT research and perspectives: "On a broader, ethical level, excluding queer perspectives and knowledges from our classrooms and our literature is, in effect, a way of enforcing compulsory heterosexuality, which hardly seems an appropriate role for language educators and researchers" (2006b, p. 7). In addition to publishing scholarly work (e.g., 1993, 1999, 2004, 2005, 2006a, 2006b, 2009), Nelson has made the topic very vivid and immediate to many in the field through her writing and presentation of a theatrical piece about LGBT ESOL teachers, titled "Queer as a Second Language" (2002). I saw that very powerful Readers' Theater piece at the TESOL conference in Salt Lake City in 2002, and I was deeply moved, as were many others in the audience, by the poignant stories portrayed.

The few other authors who have published on sexual identity issues in ESOL/applied linguistics venues include Franeta (2001); Jewell (1998); Kappra (1998/1999, 1999); Lubetsky (1998); Nguyen and Kellogg (2005); O'Mochain, Mitchell, and Nelson (2003); Snelbecker (1994); and Summerhawk (1998). Specifically regarding pedagogy and materials on sexual identity in ESOL and other classes, useful works include Barnard (n.d.); Hart (1992); Renner (1998); and Snelbecker and Meyer (1996). There have also been a few—but very few—materials writers who have included at least some small (sometimes very small, but any mention is meaningful) attention to LGBT people and issues in ESOL student textbooks; examples include Azar (1999), Folse (1996), Thewlis (1997), and, especially, Hemmert and Kappra (2004). The Teacher's Guide to the Hemmert and Kappra textbook states that the book "makes every effort to avoid stereotypes. In doing so, *Out and About* features people of various ethnic backgrounds, women in traditionally male occupations, and non-traditional families, such as single-parent families and same-sex couples" (p. vi).

My own first foray into writing about sexual identity issues was an article on "hidden identities" in the ESL classroom, in which I discussed sexual identity, along with other identities such as those relating to religion, social class, and health (Vandrick, 1997e). I addressed the issue of whether and how students and instructors with these identities self-reveal, and the implications for those individuals as well as for the other participants in the classroom, and for classroom dynamics. I discussed the role of various participants' "passing" as members of various identities not their own. I urged teachers to be aware of the possibility that students from any or all invisible identities are in fact sitting in their classrooms. I asked that teachers "actively attempt to create classrooms where people feel safe and feel they can be open about various aspects of their lives and identities, even if they do not choose to do so" (Vandrick, 1997e, p. 157).

That same year (1997b), I published a short piece urging heterosexual teachers to take responsibility for fighting homophobia, particularly in their classrooms. I reasoned (as others have before me) that those who have any kind of privilege (even if they lack privilege in another area) have an obligation to advocate for those with less privilege in that area. I argued that

> Just as men should speak out against sexism, rather than assuming or acting as if it's "only" a woman's problem, just as whites should speak out against racial discrimination, and just as able people should speak for the rights of disabled people, thus straight people should speak publicly against homophobia. This sometimes difficult work should not be left to lesbians and gays alone. (Vandrick, 1997b, p. 23)

Then in 2001, I gave a paper at the annual TESOL Convention on "Teaching Sexual Identity Issues in University ESL Classes" (Vandrick, 2001b). In that paper, I focused very closely on the classroom, on students, on teachers, on how much or how little sexual identity was discussed in second language classrooms, and on pedagogical concerns.

In 2006, Rick Kappra and I published an article on the experiences of ESL students in their ESL classrooms (Kappra & Vandrick, 2006). The article reported on interviews with several lesbian and gay students in ESL settings. Unfortunately, although the students were studying in the very liberal San Francisco Bay area, which has a large and well-known LGBT community, students still sometimes encountered prejudice and ignorance on LGBT identities and issues.

In 2008, I gave two conference papers on sexual identity issues, one at TESOL (Vandrick, 2008b) based partly on the research with Kappra, and one at CATESOL on intersections of sexual identity and other identities, especially social class (Vandrick, 2008a).

The response to my papers and articles has been mostly positive and appreciative, for which I am grateful. One letter of support for the essay (Vandrick, 1997b) on the responsibility of heterosexuals to fight homophobia, mentioned above, was signed by 26 TESOL educators and published in TESOL's newsletter at the time, *TESOL Matters* (Anderson et al., 1997). However, two other readers of that same essay (Vandrick, 1997b) wrote very critical letters to the editor in response. One labeled my article "weird" and concluded that "no wonder so many people abroad think Americans are all crazy" (Lindstromberg, 1997, p. 21). The other, more temperate in writing style, argued that teachers should not raise political/social issues, and that doing so in some EFL settings could even be dangerous for teachers (Ford, 1997). In my response to Ford, invited by the editor (Vandrick, 1997d), I acknowledged his concerns, restating my belief that each teacher has to assess her or his own teaching site and situation before deciding which issues to address, but also reiterating my hope that those who could safely do so would be proactive on behalf of LGBT rights and equity.

Intersections of Sexual Identity and Other Identities

As briefly discussed above, and as we all know from our own experiences, we are all bundles of various identities, including but not limited to our identities related to gender, social class, race, ethnicity, sexual identity, religion, ability or disability, age, and health status. Some identities may be more salient to an individual, or to others as they respond to an individual, but no identity can completely define a person. Not only are our identities multiple, but they intersect and interact in various ways, sometimes unpredictably. Again, these intersections affect not only the individual herself or himself, but also other people as they perceive and respond to that individual. If, for example, a person has an identity that is sometimes stigmatized, negative perceptions of the person may either be made worse by his or her having another stigmatized identity, or may be lessened by her or his simultaneous possession of a more privileged identity. For example, a gay black man might find that racial prejudice and homophobia reinforce each other, causing him to be doubly discriminated against. On the other hand, gay men, like most men (but especially white men), have a certain amount of male privilege; one of the many manifestations of male privilege is the fact that men still earn substantially more money, on average, than women, lesbian or straight, do. Or a lesbian or gay man of a privileged social class may be protected by that privilege from some of the negative experiences a lesbian or gay man of working-class background might experience. For example, a gay man with economic and social privilege may be able to choose to live in a geographical area where there is less heterosexism and homophobia. He may be able to afford to have protections such as living, working, shopping, and socializing in "safe" neighborhoods.

Illustrating the intersections of various identities, and therefore the interlocking responsibilities we all have, William G. Tierney discusses commonalities and differences between oppression of LGBTs and other minorities such as African Americans, and concludes that

> as members of an oppressed group, we have an obligation to learn about the Other and not simply confine our concerns and analyses to our own specific background. In particular, white gay men who hold economically powerful positions in society have an obligation to understand how the economy functions to provide privileges to some and deny other individuals basic economic justice. (1997, p. 89)

Tierney makes the point that even within an oppressed group, some have more power and privilege than others, and should use that privilege to support those without, and to work for change. So, for example, those in academe, queer or straight, with tenure and seniority can be more active in working for the rights of LGBTs than those without such security.

In the ESOL setting, it may be, for example, that a gay international ESOL student studying in the United States who attends an institution in a more liberal area, and who has money to live in a safe place, will likely be less vulnerable to discrimination and perhaps harm than a poorer immigrant student studying and living in a less progressive area.

Although I am interested in connections among all identities, I am particularly interested here—as I am throughout this book—in the influence of social class. Sexual identity and social class are intimately connected (Raffo, 1997). How do these two identities interface? Is it easier for LGBTs who are middle class or upper middle class than it is for working class LGBTs to come out and feel safe because of their education and professional standing? It is important that sexual identity be considered in the context of various types of oppression, including class oppression; Field (1995) asserts that "gay oppression cannot be fought on a separate battleground from the central war against class oppression" (p. 30). Dews and Law (1998) discuss intersections of class and sexual identity, especially working class and lesbian and gay identities, in the context of experiences of students and faculty in higher education settings. They assert that "coming out for lesbian and gay young people from the working class is . . . very different from coming out for lesbian and gay young people from professional/managerial-class families" (p. 8). They believe it is much harder for working-class youth, partly because they did not have models of working-class lesbians and gays; they "grew up imagining that only middle- and upper-class people were allowed the luxury of being gay: famous artists, rich eccentrics, writers and poets" (p. 9).

Age also intersects with sexual identity and social class identity. (For more on age, see Chapter 10.) In some cases coming out, or being comfortable about one's sexuality, may come more easily to older people because of their knowledge and experience. But nowadays younger people, at least in parts of the world, have grown up in times when there is more openness about sexual identity, and thus may be more likely to be accepting of their own or others' minority sexual identities. Again, social class privilege makes a difference. I think of a friend's son, a young man who grew up in the San Francisco Bay area, attended elite and fairly progressive private schools, graduated from an Ivy League college, and now lives in another liberal large city. This young man is gay, and has been able to be quite open about his sexual orientation, because he has always been in privileged and progressive locations and situations. In fact, my friend is concerned that because he has been protected by these types of privilege, he may be unprepared for the experiences he may well have at some point with people who are prejudiced against LGBTs, and could denigrate or even harm him.

Cultural differences are also a factor. For example, it is likely much easier for students from Western Europe than from many other areas to be open about their sexuality because European societies tend to be more open about sexual identity. In some parts of the world, there is an explicit denial of, and/or prohibition against, minority sexual identities. For example, in September 2007, Mahmoud Ahmadinejad, President of Iran, stated in a speech at Columbia University that there was no homosexuality in Iran. Yet we know that (of course) there are gay men and lesbians there, as there are everywhere; in fact, LGBTs in Iran have been punished and even executed for their homosexuality. Iran is just one of many countries where homosexuality is forbidden by both governments and religious authorities.

However, those of us who live in the United States can in no way be comfortable or smug about the way LGBT people are treated; although there are more legal protections for LGBTs than in many countries, a sizable proportion of the United States population still believes that homosexuality is wrong. Many of these people derive their anti-homosexual beliefs from their religions. Christianity, the largest religion by far in the United States, is very divided about this issue, as are other religions in the United States and elsewhere. Furthermore, members of the political right wing in the United States have used sexual identity issues for their own purposes. For example, they have vociferously attacked same-sex marriage and used it as a "wedge" issue to distract voters from more central issues such as the war in Iraq and the huge economic gap between the rich and the poor, a gap that is even further exacerbated by the current economic crisis in the United States and worldwide.

Perhaps most of all, sexual identity intersects with gender identity. As discussed in the introduction to this chapter, part of the definition of sexual identity actually includes gender identity, as in the case of transgendered people who feel that their birth sex does not agree with their perception of their own gender. Much of the population has little understanding of this mismatch, and those who do not behave according to gender expectations of "normality" are often harassed and even harmed. In a tragic incident in 2008, for one of many examples, a 15-year-old gay male high school student in Oxnard, California, who often came to school dressed in feminine clothing and makeup, was shot to death in what police strongly suspect was a hate crime. The discomfort of many with people who do not follow their assigned gender roles is, in the case of males dressing or acting in ways that females have traditionally dressed or acted, compounded by the misogyny that still exists in most societies. Students in ESOL classes, like students elsewhere, sometimes mock gay men as effeminate and lesbians as masculine; apparently, not fitting assigned gender roles is still derided, and can bring harm to those not conforming with the "proper" roles and behavior for their gender.

Clearly, we cannot look at sexual identity or any other identity without looking at contexts. We have to take into account the other identities of each individual, and the other identity factors in society, whether they are related to social class, religion, political beliefs, age, culture, gender, or any other identity.

Concerns about Representation of Others

As I briefly discussed in the introductory chapter of this book, when one speaks or writes about identities of others, one must always be concerned about representation. Because I often do speak and write about others' identities, as I am doing in this chapter, I am concerned, like many scholars (e.g., Fine, Weis, Weseen, & Wong, 2000), about whether I am qualified to speak "for" those with identities different than my own; it seems presumptuous to do so. I wonder if I have enough knowledge, and I worry that I will appear condescending, as if I appear to consider myself a kind, helpful outsider stepping in to "help" those with minority or stigmatized identities. Because I am female, I do not feel this concern when I write about gender, especially the issues that women face, but I do feel it when I write about race, sexual identity, and disability, among other identity issues, because in each of those cases, I write from the position of the majority, or at least from the position of the group that generally possesses power and privilege in that context.

One issue of representation to keep in mind is the danger of essentializing. Not all people with a certain identity have certain characteristics. In addition, as discussed above, each person has multiple identities, and should not be limited to being discussed or represented as if she or he merely embodies one of those identities. Another issue regarding representation is the idea of giving voice to those who do not have a way to represent themselves. On the one hand, each person, and people of various identities, obviously should have their own opportunities to speak for themselves, to tell about their own experiences. On the other hand, sometimes, as I discussed earlier when speaking about the obligation to advocate for other identities than one's own, people with certain identities cannot speak out for and about themselves, at least at certain times and in certain places; their environments or cultures may make it difficult and even dangerous to do so. Especially when this is true, it is important for others to speak out, but only after educating themselves and while making every effort to be accurate and transparent in doing so.

These concerns about representation have been ongoing for me, as I know they are for others. Lately I have been finding it helpful to think about the prepositions used with the word "speak." I feel uneasy about speaking "for" groups of which I am not a member, just as I may not want others to speak "for" groups of which I am a member, such as men speaking "for" women. But perhaps I can speak "with," "about," and "out for" those groups, just as I hope that others will do for groups of which I am a member, especially women.

By speaking "with" members of a minority group, such as LGBTs, I can learn more about the (obviously varied rather than monolithic) issues, problems, and views of members of the group. I have tried to do this with LGBT colleagues. I can, in addition, offer myself as an ally, and ask LGBT colleagues and friends how they would like interested others to proceed in order to be helpful educators and advocates. For example, at a TESOL convention a few years ago, when I expressed my concerns to a lesbian academic about appearing to speak for LGBTs, she told me that my concerns were valid, but she encouraged me to continue speaking and writing about sexual identity topics, convincingly assuring me that LGBT people need and want allies. I like the word "allies," which seems to encapsulate the role of heterosexuals who see inequities and want to work against them.

After speaking with LGBTs (or other groups not one's own), and educating oneself about the issues, one can speak "about" the group; in other words, one can educate others, especially others of the majority group, in this case heterosexuals. One can share information and promote awareness; after all, this is the job of an educator.

Finally, one can speak "out for" minority groups, meaning that one can advocate for equal rights and justice for groups that are not currently receiving those rights and that justice. This speaking out could take place in our classrooms and institutions, in family situations, in political venues, or wherever we have contacts and possibly influence. It can be general, or it can be specific support of students, colleagues, and other people we know who are experiencing bullying, hazing, shunning, or other forms of unfair treatment and discrimination.

This focus on "speaking with," "speaking about," and "speaking out for," as opposed to "speaking for," perhaps seems simplistic or too schematic, but I offer it as a way to at least tentatively approach the dilemma I feel, and I believe many of my heterosexual colleagues may feel, about wanting to be supportive and to advocate for our LGBT colleagues and students, but being afraid of missteps.

As I come to the end of this description of my own "journey" (so far), both personal and professional, regarding sexual identity, I hope that my stories and reflections may encourage others, of any sexual identity, in education, especially TESOL and second language education, to consider their own roles in addressing sexual identity issues and in being supportive of our students and colleagues.

A dozen years after my first classroom vignette, the story told at the beginning of this chapter, I make sure that LGBT issues, along with other social issues, are regularly addressed in my classes. In contrast to the nervous silence or giggles of past students, my current students are generally more knowledgeable, more interested, and more willing and even eager to read about, ask about, and discuss the issues. I do not naïvely believe that prejudices have been erased, but I see signs of hope, signs of change.

Chapter *8*

On Beginning to Write at 40[1]

Note to the Reader:

I include this essay as it is one of the three (along with those published in this book as Chapters 2 and 4) of my previous publications that incorporate personal narrative. Like the other two essays, this one is important to me because it allowed me to explore aspects of my academic life through a combination of sharing my own experience and showing how that experience reflected larger issues in our field. This piece has real emotional weight for me, because it describes my difficult and long-delayed path to writing and publishing. Writing this piece was both painful and cathartic for me; however, I would not publish it only for that reason if I did not feel that it also speaks to the issues and obstacles experienced by many other academics, especially in TESOL and related fields, and especially women.

[1] This essay was originally published as Vandrick, S. (2003). On beginning to write at 40. In C. P. Casanave & S. Vandrick (Eds.), *Writing for scholarly publication: Behind the scenes in language education* (pp. 53–60). Mahwah, NJ: Lawrence Erlbaum Associates. Copyright 2003 from *Writing for scholarly publication: Behind the scenes in language education,* edited by Christine Pearson Casanave and Stephanie Vandrick. Reproduced by permission of Taylor & Francis Group, LLC, a division of Informa plc.

I have always been an avid, even addicted, reader, and I have always been in love with words and language. I have always loved the academic world, the world of the university campus, of classes, of the library, of scholarly and intellectual discussions and pursuits. Thus although throughout high school and college I had little idea of what I wanted to do with my future, it gradually became clear that of course that future had to include books, ideas, and campuses. As a new graduate assistant in the English Department at the age of 21, I was assigned to teach English as a Second Language (ESL), and after my first day of teaching, I knew that teaching at the college level would be my career. I pursued that career and have taught ESL and other subjects (literature, Women's Studies) my whole adult life. But I didn't begin seriously writing for scholarly publication until I was 40. Before that, I wrote some short pieces, some newsletter articles, some reviews, but not a lot. I was in writing, as I have been in other parts of my life, a late-bloomer.

Why Didn't I Write Earlier?

A primary reason that I didn't write earlier was the difficult working conditions during my first 15 years of full-time teaching. Although I have been teaching ESL (and other areas) at the college level my whole adult life, my teaching situation during my first 15 years was one that did not encourage, and in fact actively discouraged, research and writing. I worked under very negative conditions at my institution, both at the department level and at the university level. ESL was considered a service field, and ESL instructors were expected to teach a heavier-than-normal load, attend many meetings, do quasi-administrative work, work on curricula, organize social events, and in general put in long hours. Efforts to do research were actively discouraged; for instance, teachers (including me, on at least two occasions) who asked to teach a certain class again in order to follow up on initiated research were purposely assigned to completely different classes. Although we were full-time faculty, and grateful for that status, we suffered many of the indignities that part-time faculty in our, and other, fields so often face: heavier teaching loads than other faculty had, desks in a shared room rather than private offices, no individual telephones, no access to research or travel funds, low status. Even worse than the specifics of this negative situation was the hostile attitude of the administrators at the time; they not only did not attempt to improve working conditions, but thought that the conditions were perfectly appropriate for the faculty, and believed that the faculty should be grateful for having their jobs and should not complain.

I can't begin to describe the pain that this difficult and hostile work situation caused my colleagues and me. It was difficult for me, as someone who had had a happy, secure childhood, to believe that people could behave in this way. I had been raised to think that if a person did her or his job well, she or he would be valued. I had always thought that people were basically good, and generally treated each other decently. I honestly couldn't comprehend cruel, manipulative motivations and behavior, and was shocked to observe it and to be its target. Still worse was to observe it in people with power over my colleagues and me. Even today, when I have been in an infinitely better situation for many years, I sometimes realize how much that time in my life affected me. Just recently, when the subject happened to come up during a conversation with a new colleague at a professional conference, I found myself choking up and briefly unable to continue speaking.

Readers may wonder why I didn't simply leave this toxic situation; I am sure some of my friends wondered the same thing at the time. Perhaps I should have left then. Yet leaving a full-time university position in ESL, in a premier geographical location, especially knowing of the scarcity of such positions, made it very hard to leave. I also had family and roots in the area. After moving often during my childhood, I didn't want to keep moving as an adult. And perhaps I was just plain insecure about looking for a new job.

All of these conditions interacted with my own lack of confidence in myself as a scholar and researcher. Some of the reasons for this had to do with my own personality, and some had to do with gender. Some had to do with the internalization of others' regard of ESL as a second-class field. Although intellectually I did not and do not believe these belittling conceptions about my field, all the stereotypes insidiously seeped into my mind, as I know they do, unfortunately, for many teachers in our field: *ESL is only remedial, anyone who speaks English can teach English, you are "only" dealing with "foreigners," ESL is not a real discipline.*

Other less personal factors that made me less likely to write were the facts that twenty-five years ago, there were far fewer scholarly journals in the fields of ESL/Applied Linguistics, and far fewer faculty in full-time university positions in TESOL/Applied Linguistics; therefore, except for a few prominent scholars at a few institutions, there was not much of a "culture" of expectation of writing and publishing. In addition, most of the writing and publishing that was done was on topics related to linguistics and language learning. As a person who came to ESL through my interests in literature, language, and culture, my focus was more on literature and on sociopolitical issues than on, for example, second language acquisition research. I thought that in order to write, I would have to do quantitative research, use statistical analysis, and write about, for instance, how language learners acquired a certain grammatical competence.

Readers may also wonder whether I was and am just using the difficult situation at my institution as an excuse for why I didn't write. I myself have wondered this at times. Sometimes I thought, and think, that if I had only been more motivated, more disciplined, harder working, more confident, I could have and should have written anyway, despite the difficult work setting. Perhaps it is true that I could have and should have done more anyway. But I was not strong enough to surmount the difficulties. I need at least a bit of support and encouragement from my professional community, or at the very minimum a neutral setting rather than a destructive one, in order to write.

What Changed?

What allowed me to start writing and publishing at 40? First, much of the unhappy situation at work changed quite radically. Our university's faculty union was instrumental in fighting for better working conditions. A new administration, and in particular a new dean, had a very supportive attitude, and followed through with tangible support. For example, the ESL faculty's teaching load was reduced to the same as that of other college faculty, and in some cases, including mine, it was later further reduced to allow for research and writing time. For another example, I was finally assigned a private office, with my own telephone, computer, windows, and lock on the door. As Virginia Woolf famously said, people—and in particular women—need "a room of one's own" in order to think and write (Woolf, 1929/1959). In addition, a close colleague and friend became department chair, and she was tremendously encouraging and supportive of my writing.

I particularly remember a meeting that my colleagues and I had with our new dean, the supportive dean I mentioned earlier. He told us that he would immediately reduce our teaching load to the same load that all faculty at our university had. But, he said, we would then be expected to do the same kind and quantity of research as other faculty were expected to do. I remember experiencing a tiny moment of panic, and then a bracing rush of optimism and confidence. This was a moment of epiphany: I suddenly realized that this was the moment I had been waiting for. YES, I told my dean. Yes, of course, I would do that research and writing. No problem. Where did that confidence come from? Apparently it had been lurking underneath the surface, waiting for the opportunity to come out. It was a moment of hope and joy for me.

Simultaneously, partly as a result of the increased respect for me and my profession shown by the university, and the increased support the university gave me, I began to believe in myself as someone who could share her ideas with others by writing. Until then, on some level I had thought of writing and publishing as something that others did, others who somehow knew more, knew the magic inside information that allowed one to write and publish. Now a shift happened in me which allowed me to picture myself as, at least potentially, one of those people: a writer who publishes.

It is hard to know whether this shift was mostly a result of age, or a result of the earlier-mentioned external factors, or some combination of the two, some alchemy brought about by their interaction. Perhaps, too, I was experiencing that burst of creativity that one often sees, these days, among women at midlife. Women in general tend to be "late-bloomers" compared with men; whether this is inherent in females, socially constructed (see, e.g., Rubin, 1979), or simply a matter of the logistics of managing a family life along with a career (see, e.g., Apter, 1993; Hochschild, 1997) are knotty questions that feminists and others have not yet resolved. In any case, I know many women writers, artists, actors, musicians, photographers, and others who didn't fully come to their creative work until their forties or even later. Perhaps they were too busy with their jobs and families earlier; perhaps they lacked confidence and were not expected or encouraged to give themselves the time and opportunities to work on their art earlier. For whatever reason, I believe I am just one of many who are part of this phenomenon of late-blooming creative women.

Connected to this midlife "flowering" is the sense that most people, women or men, have: the sense that time is running short and is not as inexhaustible as one thought when one was twenty or even thirty. I am someone who tends to put things off, thinking I will do a given project "someday." But I realized at 40 that my "somedays" were not unlimited, and I started to feel that if I were ever to write, it should be soon.

And although these other factors were all preparing the ground, so to speak, I did have another definite, sudden, and distinct epiphany one day: I suddenly realized that I did not have to force myself to become interested in a linguistic topic that I didn't really have knowledge about or interest in, but that I could write about the topics I was most interested in: sociopolitical issues such as gender, class, and identity. Prior to that "epiphany," I had thought of those topics as very important to me and to my teaching, but never thought of them as topics to write about for presentation and publication in professional arenas.

With great excitement, I embarked on my first full-length article, one that took the position that it was important for teachers to act on their social and political beliefs, and not try to keep them out of the classroom. This article was published (Vandrick, 1992), and I went on to write about gender and pedagogy, class and privilege, literature in the writing classroom, and other topics close to my heart.

A Sense of Urgency

Another turning point for me, soon after I wrote and published that first full-length article in a refereed journal, came in the spring semester of 1994, when I had a sabbatical. I was determined to use the precious sabbatical time to move forward with my still very new writing career. I decided to write about critical pedagogy and ESL, a topic that was important to me. As I started reading and researching, I found myself drawn more particularly to feminist pedagogy. I knew I had found "my subject." After all, I had been a feminist since high school days, and I often taught women's issues in classes, gave lectures to international students and others on feminist issues, and considered my feminism an important part of my personal, political, and academic life. As with the first article, described earlier, I felt a great sense of excitement and "rightness" about this topic. With enthusiasm and dogged determination as well, I read every book and article I could find about feminist pedagogy, and eventually wrote several pieces on various aspects of the topic.

During that 1994 sabbatical, I found that I could work best in my office at the university, and that although there were distractions to avoid there, the distractions were fewer and less pressing than those at home. Besides, I had all my necessary materials around me in that office: my books, my files, my computer; the university library was nearby and convenient as well. I had the sense that time was very valuable, and that

I wanted to *use* my one semester sabbatical well. After all, there was an increasing urgency now that I was 44 years old.

My resolve was badly tested that semester, as a series of events made it hard for me to move forward. Renovation was being done on our building, and twice I had to move out of my office temporarily. Throughout that semester, there was noise from jackhammers and from workers yelling to each other; dirt and dust invaded my office; I felt unsettled. But nothing could stop me at that point. I just kept right on working, though complaining loudly and often. Out of that sabbatical came several publications, most notably two publications on feminist pedagogy, that I felt pleased with and that were well received (Vandrick, 1994a, 1995b).

I write about these difficulties, and my overcoming them, in order to indicate the urgency I felt at that point in my writing life. I felt desperate about preserving my time and my forward momentum; I feared the time somehow being stolen from me, or evaporating before I knew it, and I just couldn't let that happen. I also felt a great joy in writing, and that helped to keep me moving forward despite the moves and noise and dust. After all, such distractions and inconveniences were nothing compared with the psychic and logistical obstacles I had experienced for so many years in the past.

As I wrote and my articles began to be accepted for publication, and as I got some positive feedback from colleagues/readers, I became more confident about my right to speak, to write, to "join the conversation." This sense of being part of the professional conversation was immensely joyful for me. And this confidence helped me, in turn, to continue writing and publishing.

Also of great help to me has been my research group, consisting of two colleagues and me; we have, for about ten years, met regularly to talk about our writing. We have written several articles and a book together, and we read and respond to each other's individual writing as well. We encourage each other, support each other, console each other when rejection letters arrive, and celebrate when invitations or acceptance letters arrive.

A Happy Ending?

This is not a completely happy story for me. I still sometimes mourn the years in which I could have been and perhaps should have been writing. The experience of writing and publishing and being part of the professional conversation is one that feels so "right" that I wish I had begun much earlier. I blame certain conditions and even certain people for holding me back. And sometimes I blame myself for not managing to write despite the obstacles. But, as a colleague said to me, I need to remind myself that all those years were not wasted regarding writing. All the reading, teaching, thinking, discussing, and experiencing I did during those years nourishes the writing I am doing now. Maybe I wasn't ready earlier. Maybe I didn't really have a lot to say earlier. In any case, the past is the past, and it is useless and even destructive to waste energy bemoaning it.

And I have discovered that there are some advantages to coming to writing late. My life experiences and thinking certainly enrich my current writing. And because writing for publication came hard and late to me, I do not take for granted the conditions that allow me to write, and the satisfaction and pleasure of writing and of having other people read and respond to my ideas. Incidentally, my publications also helped me to get a promotion, which is certainly a result that I celebrate, but truly this happy result was almost beside the point compared with the gratification and fulfillment I have experienced since I began to be a writer. And an important byproduct has been that as a writing teacher, I can finally feel that I am practicing what I preach to my students!

This is also not a completely happy story in terms of its implications for others in our field. Here I tell my personal story in the hope that it may be encouraging to those in our field who, like I did, may feel that only "others" are qualified to write, or feel that since they haven't started yet, it is probably too late to start. When I first thought about writing this chapter, this was the major message that I wanted to convey. My narrative had a rather traditional arc, with the main character (me!) overcom-

ing tremendous obstacles to triumph in the end. But upon reflection, I
realize that the story and its implications are much more complex than
that. I do not want this to be a naïve story about how "anyone can do it,"
because I know that despite my earlier difficulties, I have been fortunate
to have many factors in my life and my professional setting that (eventually) gave me the luxury of writing: a full-time job, tenure, supportive
administration and colleagues, reasonable teaching load, private office,
computer and computer support, and funds for travel to conferences,
among others. And many other teachers in our field, perhaps even most
others, do not have these positive conditions.

So I am now conveying a very mixed, inconclusive message. On the
one hand, I want to say that if writing and publishing is your dream,
don't give up; it is never too late; you too can do it. But on the other
hand, if what allowed me to write and publish, finally, was mainly a
change in my academic situation, and in the time and support and status
and facilities available to me, then what does this say to people in our
field who do not have access to these resources? What about the many
in our field who have part-time positions, or full-time positions with
no or low rank or security, teach a heavy workload, do not have private
offices or technological resources and support, do not have funds available to attend professional conferences, and do not have support from
their administrators and institutions?

I realize that my originally intended message is in fact naïve, in that it
suggests that one must overcome adversity on one's own in order to succeed. In fact, the obstacles that were at least partially responsible for my
not writing for so many years were and are endemic to our profession;
they are institutional and societal obstacles. They are closely tied to the
low status of the field of ESL, as well as to the continuing low status of
any field in which women practitioners predominate. The way that these
obstacles have cut off many valuable voices is a real loss to our field, as
well as to the individuals whose voices have been silenced.

What message, then, can I salvage from my story? One point that I
can still legitimately and sincerely make is that age itself need not be a

factor. In other words, because one has not written and published at a younger age does not mean one cannot do so at an older age. In that sense, at least, it really is never too late. I do believe that sharing one's ideas and expertise through writing is within the grasp of many people who may feel it is not, especially those who feel this way because they feel that they are too old, and that it is too late. I would like very much to encourage those people to take the leap of faith and begin.

And the other message I would like to convey is to women faculty who have been too intimidated to write for our field's journals and publishers. Although many women in our field do write and publish, they do not do so in proportion to the number of women who teach ESL; women are underrepresented in our publishing venues. The same situation can be found in other (also generally low-prestige) fields in which women dominate: composition, education, nursing, and so on. So I urge my colleagues, particularly female colleagues, in TESOL not to be intimidated, not to believe that only "others" have the necessary ability, knowledge, and connections to publish their work. I urge that my colleagues, however old they are, take heart and plunge in.

Chapter *9*

The Power of Writing Groups

*F*our women professors, from four different disciplines, form a writing support group; we gather once a month, sometimes in a café but more often in K's sun-filled apartment, overlooking the campus yet feeling far away from campus life, to talk about our writing. There is a warm, convivial, supportive feeling in the air. After initial greetings, the choosing of drinks and snacks, the exchange of personal and campus news, we settle down and each takes a turn describing her current writing. What is she working on? What successes has she had? What failures? What problems? How is she finding time to write, and to use that time well? The others, after listening attentively, ask questions and offer advice and encouragement. When writing is not going well for one person, the rest of us provide sympathy and practical assistance; when things are going well, we celebrate each other's successes. We help each other strategize about our writing and about our careers. How does one get past a writing block? What is the best way to set aside time for writing, and to ensure that the time isn't interrupted? How should this one deal with negative reviews of a manuscript? How should that one work with a difficult editor? Should this one accept nomination to department chair? Should that one coordinate a special forum that is prestigious but time-

consuming? Is it time to apply for a promotion? A certain grant or fellowship? Sinking into comfortable chairs, sipping tea or wine, we focus on all of these issues, knowing we can trust each other and count on each other to share our experience and our support. When it is time to go, we leave reluctantly, but energized, as we go back to the challenges of our writing and our lives.

The seven "Sister Scholars" work at six universities in two countries. We keep up a constant flow of emails; some relate to shared projects; some detail problems, ask for advice; others celebrate triumphs, whether new jobs or publications or resolution of knotty departmental problems. We have our own running jokes. We meet at conferences when we can, doing colloquia and papers together, and sharing noisy, joyous dinners when we catch up on everyone's news. We have shared two brief writing retreats after conferences. And when my father died, I received a beautiful bouquet of flowers and messages of caring and support from the group.

Every Friday morning, several faculty members of the "Writing Warriors," sometimes five, sometimes 15, wearing comfortable clothes and toting laptops and book bags, gather in a reserved classroom to spend the day writing. Some come only for the morning, some the afternoon, some all day. The schedule provides for 45 minutes of silent writing, then 15 minutes to take a break; during that break, we often talk animatedly about our writing. The energy is both intellectual and psychological; the air is practically crackling with neurons and endorphins suffusing the room. The sight of those around us tapping at their computers, reading, marking up drafts, creates an atmosphere of community and encouragement. Occasional sounds float in from the hallway or outside the windows, but we are impervious, we are focused, we are writing!

Driving through the lovely wooded back roads of western Marin County, California, in ones, twos, and threes, fifteen College of Arts and Sciences faculty members from the university where I teach converge at a beautiful, rustic confer-

ence center overlooking Tomales Bay. There we are free from all work and home
responsibilities for a precious weekend devoted solely to writing. The energy is
palpable. We write in our own rooms, or in a large shared conference room; the
decision is each individual's. We meet for delicious meals in the lodge, happily
talking about our writing projects and progress, advising and encouraging each
other, then return to write some more.

My writing support group has been meeting for over ten years, reading and discussing articles on feminist theory and related topics, discussing our own academic writing, and providing each other with encouragement regarding that writing, and regarding the balancing act that most women academics engage in. The group of "Sister Scholars" that "meets" online in frequent group emails, as well as at conferences when we put on panels together, and connects over talk-filled, celebratory dinners, has been an entity for over seven years. I have participated in the Friday "Writing Warriors" group at my university for four years; this group provides a regular time and place to focus on writing, and in the breaks and lunchtimes, exchanges of information and advice. I have recently participated in several weekend writing retreats sponsored by my college. In the past, my research group met for about 12 years, not only writing and publishing a book and several articles together, but providing each other with feedback on our individual writing. And in my personal life, my "mother's group" has been meeting for 20 years (for a description of this group, see Vandrick, 1999b), and my women's reading group has been meeting for over 30 years, reading and discussing hundreds of novels and seeing each other through job changes, marriages, divorces, children, the death of parents, and many other life events. Each of these seven groups, along with others I have participated in throughout the years, has contributed enormously to the quality of my life as a person and as an academic.

Those of us in TESOL and related fields who are fortunate enough to have academic positions whose work includes scholarship generally need and want as much support as possible. For me, writing and other groups have been a prime source of such support. I have always been part of groups, starting with informal groups of friends in high school and college, and continuing through consciousness-raising groups in the early days of the women's movement. My "groups" have been enormously important to me, both professionally and personally. Groups have an almost magic power to encourage and sustain their members. Those, myself included, who enjoy the kinds of privilege that allow and facilitate the forming of such groups are blessed indeed.

Groups throughout history have built a sense of community, whether they be quilting groups, bowling teams, or reading groups (Bellah, Madsen, Sullivan, Swidler, & Tipton, 1985). My mother's 90-year-old friend, for example, gains sustenance, company, and joy from her groups: her Bible study group and her painting group. Support groups have also been enormously helpful to people at difficult times in their lives, such as living with cancer, fighting drug or alcohol dependency, or undergoing divorce.

In this chapter, I write about the power of groups in the particular context of academic women, whether in TESOL or in other fields, and I use the term "support groups" to mean any groups that provide connection, encouragement, and practical support. I particularly focus on groups that help academic women to do their scholarly writing, and to balance such work with their teaching, professional service, personal lives, and other responsibilities. I use my own groups as examples to illustrate how powerful and nourishing such groups can be.

Although most academics, and probably especially women academics, want support for their writing and research practices, it may be that those in TESOL are particularly in need of it because of the frequent marginalization of the field within academe. Some years ago, a rather imperious senior History professor of my acquaintance indicated her surprise that those in TESOL published and gave conference papers, just like other academics! Although TESOL is becoming more and more professionalized, there is still more than a whiff of condescension in the way the field is treated by many in academe. In addition, there are relatively few full-time tertiary academic positions in TESOL, so those of us in those positions need both to help each other and to advocate for each other, as well as for those who do not have access to such positions. Forming writing groups is one way to do so, both with others in our field and with colleagues in other disciplines.

The Power of Groups

The power of groups is elemental. Members of groups—whether tribes, families, or residents of a village—have always known that they can succeed better as part of groups than as individuals. We are all members of various groups without even thinking about it: our communities, neighborhoods, workplaces, children's schools, places of worship, clubs, and social groups. In the case of academics, we generally identify with our departments or programs, the larger groups formed by our colleges/ schools and universities, and our professional organizations.

Here I focus on more specific, and generally self-selected, groups, and how they have been a source of strength and productivity to academics. Many writers acknowledge the contributions that their groups, particularly their writing groups, have made to their publications and to their professional success. Laurel Richardson, a professor of sociology and women's studies, in the acknowledgments section of her book *Fields of Play: Constructing an Academic Life,* mentions with gratitude the support and assistance provided by four different writing/reading groups: the Women's Poetry Workshop, the Feminist Post-Modern Studies (PMS) reading group, the Cakes for the Queen of Heaven group, and Sociologists for Women in Society (SWS) (1997). Just reading this very particular (and slyly humorous) list makes me joyful about the array of groups available for academic women to be nourished by.

Although many groups are created by the members themselves, more and more institutions are also recognizing the helpful role that writing and reading groups can play in forwarding the research and publications of faculty, especially junior faculty, and are sponsoring such groups on campus. Many of these are offered through campus writing centers; in addition to assisting student writers, these centers now offer assistance to faculty as well. Online I found evidence of dozens of such groups (e.g., writing groups at Michigan State University, Indiana University, California State University–Fullerton, and the University of Iowa Carver College of Medicine, and reading groups at Yale University, Carleton College, and the University of Oregon). One group at Western Carolina University calls itself a "writing circle," and participants share drafts and provide each other with feedback (Hall, Mueller, & Stahl, 2003). There are, as well, many less formal groups formed by faculty themselves.

One documented example of an academic group in TESOL education, one that provided support both for teaching and writing, is described by Suhanthie Motha (2006). Motha's dissertation research included a focus on "the challenges faced by beginning K–12 ESOL teachers in the United States as they grappled with the significance of their own racial identities in the process of negotiating the inherent racialization of ESOL in their language teaching contexts" (p. 495). As part of this research, Motha held regular gatherings with four teachers; the form of these meetings was "afternoon teas." The group met in Motha's home over tea and refreshments, and discussed their teaching and other professional experiences; this format allowed the group to develop a close community that supported not only Motha's research, but the teaching and professional lives of the individual members of the group. Motha and some colleagues have since formed a writing group of early-career academic women in TESOL, calling the group "The Quotable Quills." These examples illustrate one important point about groups: there is no single template for success, as each group will adapt to the needs and wishes of the specific participants in their specific setting. Each group needs to decide when, how often, and where to meet; who the participants will be; whether the group will be open to newcomers or not; and the structure of meetings, among other decisions. My own groups, outlined above, share some common characteristics, but each is also unique.

How, specifically, do groups help academics, and in particular academic women?

First, they provide support. There is something intrinsically supportive about meeting regularly with a group of people in a similar situation, seeing that others are dealing with similar concerns and struggles, sharing problems and solutions, and giving and receiving advice and encouragement. This support can be focused on a specific project, or it can be more general. Although groups limited to one project are helpful, the level of trust and understanding that builds up over time is invaluable for those who are members of ongoing groups.

One particular type of support is feedback, both specific to a project, and in general about one's writing agenda, one's choices of which topics and writing projects to focus on, and one's difficulties writing, among other issues. The writing group I belong to, for example, always begins our meetings with a "checking-in" period when we each tell the others what we are working on, how it is going, difficulties we are encountering, and successes we have experienced. Sometimes we address personal issues as well, both on campus and off, as we are well aware that such issues affect our writing lives, sometimes profoundly. Sometimes a specific suggestion can be extremely helpful, whether it be about the direction a written piece is taking, or a tip about ways to keep on track with one's writing. Here is one small example: A few years ago when I was invited to write a book for a prestigious series, I eagerly agreed; however, for various reasons, I never seemed to be able to truly engage with writing that book. Eventually, over a period of time, my writing group helped me to see that the book was not the one I truly wanted to write, and that although I was very flattered by the invitation, I felt that there was another book (this one!) that I most wanted to put my time and energy into.

Groups can also provide specific information and ideas. Particularly when groups are interdisciplinary, they provide a sort of intellectual cross-fertilization that can be very fruitful. In several of my groups, members have suggested books and articles that related to another member's research, shared information on grants and fellowships, and offered suggestions regarding theoretical or other intersections among the disciplines they represent.

In addition, groups can provide inspiration and encouragement. Writing can be lonely and frustrating. Many of us have insecurities about our writing. Sometimes it is hard to find the time or energy to write. For all these reasons, we often need trusted colleagues to listen to us vent, to encourage us, to nudge us along, to share stories and advice, and to inspire us to continue. The regular meetings of my writing group, for example, keep me focused and on task, or when I am discouraged, give me motivation to continue. A weekend writing retreat once helped me in a different way: I had had a sort of writer's block for some time, and the one weekend of dedicated time and freedom from all other responsibility jumpstarted my writing and helped me get back on track.

Sometimes the assistance a group provides is very practical. In all my writing groups, we often talk about logistics: What kind of schedule works best for you? Do you write in the morning or evening, weekdays or weekends? How do you keep writing when you are so busy with teaching and all the other demands of work and life? Do you write at home or in your office? Can you write when you just have a few minutes to spare, or do you need long stretches of uninterrupted time? How do you ensure that you are not interrupted? How do you make sure that others—at home and on campus—respect the times you have carved out for writing? At what point do you ask others to read your drafts? At what point do you talk with editors about possible publication? Should this piece be a conference paper, an article, or a chapter in a book? Should you spend more time on getting articles submitted and published, or focus on a book? How do you ask your deans or other administrators for support? What kinds of assistance can or should you ask for? How do you deal with feeling guilty about spending time on writing when others clamor for your time and attention; on the other hand, how do you deal with feeling guilty about not spending enough time on your writing? Very recently, for one of many examples, one faculty member in the Friday "Writing Warriors" group gave another one very specific and helpful advice on shaping her book proposal, advice that helped the second member get a book contract with a prestigious publisher.

Long-Term Groups versus Short-Term Groups

So far I have been writing about ongoing, open-ended groups that meet regularly over a long, sometimes very long, period of time. But different groups have different lifetimes. Some go on for many years, as most of mine have. Others end, or simply fade away, after a time. In some cases this is because the group is no longer serving the purpose it did in the past, or because individual members move on, physically or in other ways, or because the members diverge in their interests. Occasionally, there are tensions within the group that make the experience less productive than in the past. In any case, the fact that the group has ended does not mean that it wasn't valuable during the time that it existed. The research group that I was part of for 12 years, and that produced a book (Hafernik, Messerschmitt, & Vandrick, 2002) and several articles and conference papers, and provided tremendous support and assistance for each participant's individual academic work, came to a natural ending when one of the three of us retired. We are still in close touch and still take an active interest in each other's work, but the formal portion of our group identity and regular meetings has ended; the group had its time, and that time came to a natural, graceful end.

In other cases, groups are from the beginning envisioned as existing for a limited time frame. As academics, we often find ourselves in short-term or ad hoc groups, generally focusing on specific projects with deadlines. For example, pairs or groups of academics at the same or at different institutions often join to plan conference panels, organize workshops, or produce edited volumes or special issues of journals. Such a group does not necessarily qualify as a "support group" as I have been defining such groups here, but it may, in fortunate cases. A very happy and productive group collaboration for me was working on an edited volume with a wonderful co-editor and a talented and congenial group of contributors (Casanave & Vandrick, 2003b). Of course the bulk of the common work was with my co-editor, and she and I formed a strong bond that has continued to this day, as we still discuss our work together—usually by email but sometimes by telephone or in person—and give each other feedback and encouragement. The contributors to the edited book joined us in forming a temporary community over a period of about three years from idea to post-publication. We editors kept in close touch with the group by email and at conferences, trying to make sure everyone knew exactly what was happening, and sharing drafts as we went along. Various subsets of us organized conference panels based on the book's themes, had lunches and dinners together at conferences, and in general fostered a sense of community. Several contributors told us that this experience was far better than other experiences they had had as contributors to books or conference panels; we made communication, connections, and community a priority, and we were pleased with the results, both in terms of professional conversations and connections, and in terms of how the book turned out.

Another type of short-term but productive group that I have experienced is the semesterly weekend writing retreats that my college has recently inaugurated and sponsored. Faculty apply to the retreat, describing the writing projects they are working on, and then, if accepted, attend a Friday to Sunday retreat at a conference center located in a scenic area about an hour from campus. Each faculty member has a private room, and can choose to write in that room or in a common room dedicated to writing. All meals are provided, and the conversations at meals generally focus on participants' writing projects and progress. The opportunity to have concentrated, uninterrupted time to work, in a beautiful, stress-free setting, with no responsibilities for grading papers, planning classes, making meals, answering phones, or any of the normal duties of daily life, is a much appreciated gift. At the retreats I have attended, I have done more writing over those weekends than I had for some weeks before. During meals and breaks we talked about issues we were struggling with, from substantive matters of content and structure to logistical matters. We spoke of difficulties with finding time to write, with writer's block, and with balancing our teaching, service, writing, and personal responsibilities. In some cases, very specific suggestions were enormously helpful. One writer, for example, was aided by the simple suggestion of splitting several long, unwieldy chapters into shorter ones; she immediately went back to work with renewed excitement, and later reported to the group that the new structure made great sense and had given her a new surge of creative energy as she figured out how to restructure those chapters. In the course of the weekend together in such a lovely place, riding on the excitement of having time to do extended and focused work, and through discussing small and large writing-related matters and offering each other encouragement and advice, we built an intense sense of bonding and community. The ripple effects continue, as we see each other on campus, ask about each other's work, offer possible references or ideas, and in general cheer each other on as we pursue our scholarly work.

In-Person Groups versus Online Groups

Although meeting in person is generally preferable, very productive and close groups can also thrive online. My colleagues and I, like most academics, have found email to be enormously helpful in working together on projects and/or exchanging information, references, suggestions, and feedback on our individual projects. What works well for groups that are not in the same locales, in my experience, is a mixture of in-person and email communication. The "Sister Scholars" group I referred to earlier is a group of women scholars in applied linguistics/TESOL who are widely spread geographically. Over the past several years, we have worked together on various projects, including a collective writing project (Lin et al., 2004) and several conference colloquia, and also cheer on and offer resources for each other's individual projects. As indicated, we meet at conferences and sometimes give papers together; this in-person connection is important. But in order to keep closely connected all year long, between conferences we are in frequent communication by email, and occasionally by mail or telephone.

Groups and Collaboration

Although all of the groups I have alluded to provide their members with support and information, some of the examples also involved actually working on writing projects together. These examples raise the issue of professional collaboration. Some writers favor collaborative research and writing; others can't imagine such a relationship. Collaboration, resulting in co-authored publications, is valued by some institutions and disciplines, although less valued by others (for a fuller discussion of collaborative research/writing in academe, see Hafernik, Messerschmitt, & Vandrick, 1997; for a discussion of one scholar's experiences with and reflections on collaborative scholarship, see Hedgcock, 2003). I have found my collaborations with various colleagues on various writing projects to be richly satisfying. It is important to me to write many of my publications and conference papers individually, but I like the mixture of doing some work with colleagues and some on my own. Some of the benefits of collaboration are the same benefits derived from other types of groups: exchange of information and ideas, drawing on each member's individual areas of expertise, giving each other feedback on ideas and drafts, providing a regular time to meet and move forward on projects, and more. Of course actually writing together requires working much more closely together than simply meeting to talk, or to write individually at a writing retreat. Collaboration only works well if certain conditions are met, such as respect for each other, compatible working styles,

and complementary interests and strengths. Also, in a long-term collaboration such as mine with my former research group of twelve years,
the group develops a common history and a shared body of knowledge
over time; this provides a strong foundation for ongoing work.

The coming together of a long-term group on a short-term project
produces many benefits. For example, when the long-term group of
Sister Scholars focused for some weeks on preparing a conference panel,
the papers in the panel turned out to be much more closely interwoven
than those on most panels are. Too many panels are cobbled together,
based loosely around a certain theme, and result in disparate, rather
unconnected papers. In contrast, while preparing the panel in question,
our email exchanges, recommendations of articles and books, exchanges
of drafts, and prolonged sharing of thoughts resulted in an interweaving
of ideas that produced a tightly orchestrated and cohesive presentation.
Not only the specific preparation but also the intangible aspect of, again,
drawing from our history together, our respect for each other and each
other's ideas, contributed to the success of the panel.

Qualities of Successful Groups

Although each group is different, and the qualities needed for the success of each group vary, there are some common characteristics of most
successful, effective groups. First, clearly there is some kind of common
interest, whether it is a common scholarly interest or a shared attribute such as gender; often a combination of such interests and attributes will be the binding factor (e.g., women faculty of color in the
field of Applied Linguistics). A closely related factor is common goals:
group members should agree on what the group hopes to accomplish,
whether it be, for just two examples, producing an article or discussing
common issues encountered by lesbian and gay academics. Third, personal compatibility is important, especially for long-term groups. This
does not mean that everyone in the group must be similar in personality

or temperament, or that everyone needs to be close friends, but that the group members feel comfortable meeting and working with each other. Further, a high degree of openness and trust must exist in the group. It is also helpful if group members are not competitive with each other. Flexibility, understanding, and a non-judgmental attitude are all very positive attributes in group members. Finally, there are logistical matters that have to work well in order for a group to be effective. Such matters include appropriate places and times to meet (although in some cases this "meeting" may have to be largely online) and administrative/institutional support and funding (such as the administrators at my institution who have sponsored the Friday writing groups and the weekend writing retreats, providing sites, meals, and other logistical support).

Gendered Aspects of Groups

All of the groups I have been part of have consisted entirely or mostly of women. In my experience, women seem to gravitate to and appreciate groups more than men do, at least the kinds of groups I describe here. Occasionally, male faculty members have attended either the Friday writing days or the weekend writing retreats, but they don't attend regularly, and they seem to drift off after one or two meetings. Of course there are exceptions, and I do not want to essentialize by gender, but my own experiences and those of many others indicate that for whatever reasons, women are more likely to join, benefit from, and continue in various small support groups related to writing and academic life. Men may be just as likely to join large professional organizations, which provide many benefits as well, but not small writing groups.

As mentioned earlier, one of my earliest groups was one of the "consciousness-raising" groups that so many women were forming in the late 1960s and early 1970s as part of the "women's liberation" movement. Women at the time were hungry for validation of their feelings, and meeting and speaking regularly with other women fulfilled this need.

As an undated, unsigned broadsheet titled "Sisterhood and the Small Group" that I still have from that time period passionately and touchingly expresses it,

> Liberation is a constant process—and for a woman whose liberation involves . . . an end to her loneliness and isolation from other women, it would be both agonizing and impossible without their support. And to provide this support, women have organized the "small group"—the strength of our movement, through which women reach out to each other, . . . grow together. It is our best means of raising consciousness, our most effective organizing tool, and . . . our most human structure.

As always happens when one considers the role of privilege, we find that the question of women and groups is more complicated than "women like and work well in groups." Because of their various and diffuse obligations at work and at home, women may need and want the sort of enforced aspect of dedicated time for writing, and for talking about writing. Because society is still, to some extent, set up on the "husband at work, wife at home to take care of the house and children and other details of everyday life" model, working women often have greater responsibilities for home and family (although this has changed somewhat in the past 30 years, it has still not changed enough). Women also, in my experience, do the lion's share of service at their institutions, especially the kinds of service that take a lot of time but don't necessarily earn a lot of credit/recognition, such as advising and committee work that focuses on the nitty-gritty issues that must be dealt with in academe (Cummins, 2005; National Research Council, 2007; Tharenou, 1994); this is as much the case in TESOL as in other fields, and perhaps even more so. So it is hard for them (us) to find the time, and—maybe even harder—to prioritize their writing over the other things they have to do, or that others ask them to do. First, we women often have trouble saying no, and second, we often put other people's needs/wants above our own. Again, I recognize that these are generalizations, even stereotypes, but I have seen these phenomena over and over again, as have my female friends and colleagues. Men seem to have so much easier a time than women do prioritizing their own research and writing. For example, I know many more male faculty members than females who stay home several days a week to write, thereby avoiding the day-to-day issues and problems that arise in any department or program and that have to be dealt with as they come up. Most academics, but again especially women, know what it is like to have their research and writing constantly interrupted. There are meetings to attend, files to read for search committees or award committees, and recommendation letters to write. At one's office, the phone rings, emails flood in, students or colleagues stop by to ask questions or request assistance or just chat, the program assistant or other staff needs guidance, forms need to be filled out, and more. All of these "interruptions" are part of our jobs, of course, and many of these interactions are productive and even enjoyable, but they do make it difficult to set aside the chunks of time and the concentration we (at least most of us) need for writing. If one works at home, it is probably easier to work uninterrupted, but there are still interruptions—phone calls, doing a quick piece of necessary housework, maybe attending to the needs of children or aging parents. Again, most of these are good things, not bad, but they contribute to the lack of uninterrupted, dedicated time for writing. So the time provided by groups or retreats, written into one's calendar and reserved specifically for paying attention to one's writing, is valuable and valued by women academics.

Women not only tend to join groups, but also tend to turn groups into communities. The groups are functional, yes, but they serve emotional and community-building functions as well. A critical element of this community-building aspect is that women tend to blur the boundaries between the professional and the personal in these groups. I understand that this could be a negative factor in some cases, but in the vast majority of cases, in my experience, this is a positive characteristic. This is not to say in any way that women's writing groups, for example, are not serious, focused, and productive. Rather it means that women understand that our professional and personal lives are inextricably intertwined. We write well when our lives are in balance. We write well when we feel supported by our colleagues and allies. We like to be with other people who understand that we are balancing our time, responsibilities, and emotional energy among the various aspects and demands of our work, our families, and our personal lives. We are not afraid to share problems and to seek and give advice and encouragement. We do not feel that we are endangering our own success or making ourselves too vulnerable when we acknowledge problems, setbacks, or concerns. When we are in regular contact with colleagues we trust and like, writing becomes less solitary and more vital and engaging. Furthermore, as a bonus, we enjoy our interactions with our colleagues, sharing not only support but also celebration of successes and humor about the quirky unexpected aspects of the scholarly life.

The Role of Privilege

As with the other topics discussed in this book, privilege plays a role. In addition to gendered aspects of writing groups and related support groups, there are other aspects relating to privilege, aspects that play a role in determining who is able to form, sustain, and benefit from groups. It takes time, resources, and flexibility to find, form, and participate in groups. These characteristics are generally most available to those with certain types of privilege: the privileges of adequate incomes, reasonable and flexible schedules, knowledge of how to find and connect with appropriate participants, and access to meeting places and technological resources. A busy part-time instructor—such as so many in TESOL—who is teaching at two or more institutions, receiving inadequate pay and few if any benefits, and not getting any institutional support for her research or writing, is far less likely to have the time, energy, or other resources to form and attend a writing group.

In addition, a sort of intangible sense of privilege is necessary in order to form and benefit from writing support groups and other such entities: the sense that one is entitled to such "luxuries," can take advantage of them, and will not feel inferior or out of place with others in the group. So, for example, someone who teaches part-time or in a non–tenure track position, or who is new to an institution, or is in a less–prestigious field (e.g., TESOL, Composition), might feel reluctant to join such a group, let alone propose and organize it. And often others will not think to include members of these groups. The writing retreats and Friday writing days sponsored by my institution illustrate both sides of this "privilege" factor. On the one hand, those of us who participate enjoy the privilege of a supportive institution. On the other hand, only full-time faculty are invited to the retreats and writing days, so the many part-time faculty are once again marginalized.

Even less-obvious cases of the role of privilege turn out, upon examination, to be enabled by a certain amount of privilege. For example, the Sister Scholars group, which meets at conferences and online, is premised on access to funds (either from members' institutions or from their own pockets), time, and institutional permission to miss classes to attend conferences, as well as on at least basic computer equipment and technical support (again either from one's institution or from one's own resources) to enable email correspondence, exchanging and editing of drafts, and accessing articles and other resources online.

I speak of these areas of privilege not to discourage those who may want to form or join appropriate groups, but to acknowledge the role of the tangible and intangible capital that privilege provides, even in this seemingly simple arena. However, despite the difficulties I have outlined, and that I do not want to minimize, I hope that readers, in the field of TESOL or otherwise, whatever degree or type of privilege they have or lack, will consider joining or starting groups. Sometimes all it takes is someone to make it a priority, gather others together, and plan a few simple logistics regarding time and place. I am quite sure that those who do so will find it enormously helpful, nurturing, and productive.

Chapter *10*

The Aging Educator

*I*t is my first day of teaching as a very young graduate assistant. I am extremely nervous. I wonder how I, who was an undergraduate student myself just three months before, can have the authority and expertise to teach an advanced ESL writing class. It doesn't help that I am babyfaced, very young looking, nor that most of my students are graduate students and older than I am. I (over)prepare carefully and conscientiously, and the class goes well. As the class hour proceeds, I feel increasingly elated, and by the time I walk out of the classroom, I feel a sense of exaltation, a "high." This is it! This is what I was born to do!

Thirty-five years later, our program assistant tells me there is someone here to see me. I go out into the reception area and see a man of perhaps 50 years old, with a young woman of about 25 years old. He greets me enthusiastically, and reminds me that he was in one of my ESL classes about 30 years ago, when he was a very young student and I was only a bit older. He is from a Middle Eastern country, has a high position with the government there, and has brought his daughter for a visit to the United States. He tells me several times how much he *liked our program and my class, and how often he remembers his time at our university. We look at his records, and find a photograph of him looking very young; we laugh nostalgically about those days, and about how much time has passed. Neither of us remarks directly on how much we have each changed.*

Now in my late 50s, I feel myself in a somewhat unsettled zone between youthful forward movement and intimations of aging. So much in my personal and professional life has changed during the more than 35 years I have been teaching. People—family members, friends, colleagues—around me talk more of health issues, of slowing down, of possibly retiring. My parents' generation has a host of illnesses, physical and mental, and many of them are dying or have died. My father died in 2003; my mother is in reasonably good health and stays her positive and active self, but has had increasing health problems, has recently downsized from her house into an assisted living community, and watches as several of her siblings and friends ail and die. I recently took a trip with my mother to visit relatives and friends in their 80s, and although it was wonderful to see them, I felt the oppressive weight of their ailments and limitations. One aunt was in a wheelchair, her movements mostly limited to her home. My mother's college friend and bridesmaid was cheerful and active, but her mind and memory were failing badly. Soon after that trip, I happened to read in quick succession two novels (Hadley, 2007; Sebold, 2007) and a memoir (Hampl, 2007) that, by chance, all focused on aged parents and the ravages of age, which furthered focused me on the topic of advancing age and how it affects both the aging individual and those around her or him. I do not mean that I am only focusing on the negative, on illness, on death; no, I expect to have many more years of productive work and life, and I look forward to those years with zest. But I have begun to think more about the aging educator, and the changes that occur as one moves into the later stages of her or his career.

I feel the breath of time and age at my back, in both my personal and professional lives (and as we know, for academics, the two lives are closely intertwined). I still enjoy my teaching and other university work, and still feel positive about my scholarly work and writing; I believe I still have something to say, but I realize that I have less time to say it than ever before. A close colleague who is only four years older than I am retired three years ago. Two of my younger brothers recently retired from long teaching careers. Increasingly frequently, people ask me when I am thinking of retiring; when they ask, I am surprised. Who, me? I am not one of "them"—someone who is ready to move to that stage. That is years away . . . not even on my radar! And yet . . . one day I find myself calculating when my husband and I could manage financially to retire. I find myself tuning in to stories of who is retiring and when, and what they are doing with the time freed up by retirement.

I never used to read obituaries; now I do. I also find myself, especially since my father's death and the subsequent sorting through of his possessions and writings, going through my own possessions and writings, and discarding many of them. I recently reread the diaries I kept in college, and then destroyed them. I threw away many old letters. There wasn't anything seriously incriminating in those diaries and letters (although some parts were embarrassingly immature!), but I felt the need to clear away the old, the unnecessary papers in my life. I also did the same at my office, getting rid of years of old teaching materials, early drafts of articles, and other outdated materials. I realize that if I haven't used something in many years, it is unlikely I ever will again. I also made a renewed effort to make sure my affairs and papers (will, insurance, financial files, etc.) were in order. This may sound morbid, but I think it is just an indication that I finally understand, in my bones, mortality; if my father could die, so can I.

Some days I feel that my first days of teaching were just yesterday, and that I am basically the same person who started teaching so many years ago; other days I see how far I have traveled since that day, and I think about the stages I have passed through since then, as well as the later stages of life that I am approaching. I find myself reflecting on what it is to be an aging educator, and on the path I have taken to get to this point in my life and career.

My first day of teaching—the one I describe in the first scenario above—set the stage for years of feeling passionate about teaching. I had an intense relationship with the classroom, with my students, with our conversations, and with my work on a college campus. Despite having a very satisfactory "other" life as a graduate student who enjoyed her studies and her active social life, my teaching became very central. I looked forward to teaching class every day. I missed my classroom and my students over the weekends. These feelings continued as I moved into my first "real" (post-graduate school) teaching position.

At the time, I was not very analytical about the "high" I got from teaching, and in retrospect, I can see that not all my feelings were noble ones such as "contributing to education" and "helping students learn and develop." On some level, there were also less idealistic personal motives: I liked the feeling of autonomy, authority, and power. I was in charge! There was also the novelty of any new experience: I enjoyed getting to know students from all around the world. And teaching gave me a sense of pride, as I seemed to be good at it. Maybe most of all, it made me feel, finally, like an adult, with an adult life, responsibility, respect, and paycheck.

For context about my being so immediately taken with teaching, I can look to my family background and my own experiences with classrooms and education. I had always enjoyed my own schooling, and been successful at school, so I had positive feelings about classrooms and education. I came from a family of teachers, including a grandmother, a grandfather, a great-aunt, my mother, an aunt, an uncle, and two of my three brothers. I was always impressed by my grandfather; my mother had often proudly told me that he had been the Chief Inspector of Schools for a large district of the Canadian province of British Columbia. My great-aunt, too, was a longtime, well-respected teacher who was also active in the peace movement. My mother taught deaf children when I was very young, later taught "emotionally disturbed" children, and still later became a teacher educator/consultant for other special education teachers. So education was in my blood. But I hadn't grown up dreaming of becoming a teacher. I hadn't had "pretend" classes for my younger brothers, or for my dolls. Nothing had prepared me for the intensity of my response to the teaching situation.

I am now definitely a member of the "older" teachers group. I still enjoy teaching. But the intensity of the early years has lessened. Although I have been fortunate to have (mostly) good teaching situations and positions, and to have a certain amount of variety in my teaching life, the novelty is far less. There is a certain amount of repetition. In addition, I clearly have a different relationship with my students. When I started off, I was the same age as many of them; now I could be their mother (in fact, most of them are younger than my mid-20s daughter); soon I will be old enough to be their grandmother. Obviously they look at me differently, as I look at them from a different perspective. Although it is sometimes disconcerting that students see me as older than their own parents, I also find that they sometimes attribute wisdom and nurturance to me because of my age. A strange feeling I sometimes experience is that I am aging while my students are staying the same age; on the other hand, I often feel that I am standing in one place (my classroom, the university) while generations of students flow into and out of my classrooms and the university, on to their future lives.

At the risk of overgeneralizing, even stereotyping, let me sketch out descriptions of new, young teachers and, in contrast, older teachers. Young teachers tend to be enthusiastic, energetic, with many ideas of how to teach and how to make a difference in their students' lives. Sometimes they have some trepidation about teaching and its challenges, but they also tend to have the vast confidence of youth, the confidence that anything is possible. They are not jaded, so they have a kind of purity of goals and intentions about "saving" their students, and the world. They are closer to their students' ages than older teachers are. This has both advantages and disadvantages: on the one hand, they are able to remember and understand what it is like to be the age of their students, and to "relate" to those students; on the other hand, they perhaps identify too closely with the students, and may be perceived by those students as lacking experience and authority. Their relative lack of experience does, in fact, occasionally limit their teaching ability, and/or cause them to blunder in ways that more experienced teachers would not.

Older teachers (and here I mean those who have taught more than 20 years), on the other hand, obviously have more experience, knowledge, and maturity. They are perhaps at their intellectual peaks, and are able to truly integrate theory and experience. In addition to knowledge about their content matter and about pedagogy and students, they have the kind of life experience that gives them perspective, and a long view; they have experienced success and failure, love and loss, perhaps parenthood, perhaps illness, and many of the other vicissitudes that life brings us. Although students are able to "relate" to instructors near their age, some students may appreciate teachers who are parental figures; women teachers of middle age or older are often especially looked to by students for a sort of motherly nurturance. The negative side of teachers' being older may include being somewhat jaded, realizing that their youthful dreams of changing the world were perhaps grandiose and unrealistic. Sometimes, too, there is a tendency to rest on their laurels, rather than to keep putting forth maximum effort in their classes. Innovation is perhaps less a goal and less frequent in practice. There may be a feeling of weariness, a sense that one has "seen it all." Again, these are generalizations, with many exceptions.

So each age has its advantages and disadvantages for teachers, and for their students; each age allows teachers to be effective—or ineffective— in different ways. Of course we are all essentially the same people at different ages, so someone who is a good teacher when young will likely be a good teacher when older, and a "bad" teacher when young will likely not essentially change (although further education and experience can sometimes make a profound difference).

It is important to note here that broad generalizations about the qualifications of aging teachers may be dangerous for job applicants of a certain age. It is troubling to hear that older applicants are sometimes rejected because of their age. Templer (2003) writes about this phenomenon in the world of TEFL; I am sure it also happens in TESOL and other settings, despite laws that are supposed to protect against this type of discrimination. All of us will eventually be, or already are, "older" educators. A minority of TESOL professionals—and I am fortunate to be among them—have secure, tenured jobs, but a large majority of our colleagues do not. I join Templer in urging that we educators, especially those of us fortunate enough to have secure positions, pursue this issue and make efforts to end this type of discrimination against our aging colleagues.

Perceptions of myself as an aging educator affect my day-to-day teaching life in specific ways. In the classroom, when students sometimes don't understand a grammar point, or don't employ a certain writing strategy, just for a flash I sometimes, irrationally, think, "I have been teaching you this point for all these years . . . why haven't you gotten it yet?" before I come to my senses and remember that each new cohort of students is new and needs to be taught anew. When issues are raised in our program, department, or college meetings, I increasingly often think (but refrain from saying!), "Oh, this issue again," and recall all the prior discussions of the same issues over the years. When freshly minted teachers breathlessly suggest an innovation, or recount a creative class activity, one that they think is completely original but that experienced teachers have been using for many years, I bite my tongue and applaud their creativity, but also think "Been there, done that." When younger colleagues from various sectors of the university grumble about working conditions, I have to control myself not to constantly be the "voice of the past," explaining how much worse things were "in the old days." Sometimes they are kind enough to tell me they value my perspective and institutional memory, but I know enough to severely ration stories from battles past. I both take a certain pride in, and am shocked by, finding myself the oldest one in the room at many faculty or committee meetings. When did this happen?

It also strikes me that because TESOL is a young discipline, those of us who are in our fifties or older have grown up and grown older along with the field itself. Now we are reflecting on those years of maturing along with our field. Of particular interest in this vein is Blanton and Kroll's 2002 collection of essays by longtime ESL composition teachers; they state that

> [w]e find ourselves, late in our careers, looking
> back with wonder, curiosity, perhaps even wist-
> fulness, reflecting on what we have learned and
> how we might share our cumulative learning, our
> insights, with others, especially young colleagues.
> Reflecting on how we might bear witness. (p. v)

Blanton and Kroll's book also contains particularly thoughtful and pro-vocative reflections by Leki and by Blanton on how the field has grown and changed through the years, what we have learned, and what we still have to learn (Blanton, 2002; Leki, 2002). They both emphasize that we must constantly evaluate and re-evaluate our assumptions, our goals, and our teaching methods.

On the one hand, for older educators, there is the familiarity of the relatively unchanging aspects of teaching: classrooms, students, curricula, lectures, discussions, readings, essays, tests, grades, excellent students, and students with problems. In other ways, though, much has changed over the years. This is not the place for an extensive history of the TESOL field, but here I give just a few examples, taken from my own experi-ences, of how it has changed enormously over the past thirty-plus years. I remember grammar drills, and deadening assignments requiring students to repeatedly rewrite the same paragraphs in different tenses or change the first person pronouns to third person. I remember the days when lan-guage labs were quite primitive, and when we made language lab tapes by reading into the little microphone of a basic tape recorder. I remem-ber when we had no duplicating machines, only "ditto machines," which produced messy, purple copies. Technology has become more important, sophisticated, and prevalent. ESL classrooms have become more student-centered and more communicative. There has been a move to more critical approaches, to more content, to ESP (English for Specific Purposes), and to EAP (English for Academic Purposes).

As for doing our scholarly work: in the "old days" we wrote our papers on typewriters, and organized panels and coauthored works by mail and telephone (land lines, not cell phones), before the advent of email. I clearly remember when computers were esoteric machines found only in computer labs, businesses, or administrative offices, but certainly not on every faculty member's desk. There were far fewer journals and conferences in our field, and there was less pressure to publish.

Technology has been a welcome boon for both our teaching and our research/writing. It also presents challenges to older educators, for whom keeping up with the technology is often harder than it is for younger academics. Personally, I love my computers and all I can do with them, but I also feel I am always a little behind with technology, and have to push myself to go to each new step. Like most educators and parents, I am in awe of the ease with which young people seem to feel comfortable with the ever-changing technology. Regarding technology, once again privilege is a factor. Those of us who have access to good equipment, training, and tech support through our institutions are very fortunate. It gives me much peace of mind knowing that if anything goes wrong, or if I have a question about how to accomplish something with my computer or with classroom equipment, someone from the university IT (information technology) office will provide me with the assistance I need.

Another more overarching change is that the field is now more closely connected with, and influenced by, several other fields such as—besides Applied Linguistics, which it has always been connected with—Composition Studies, Literature, Sociology, and Education. A huge change in the field has been the "social turn," as evidenced in the increasing prominence of critical pedagogy, critical applied linguistics, feminist pedagogy, language policy, postcolonial studies, and other theoretical and pedagogical trends. This social turn provides quite a contrast to the period when I began teaching, and for many years after, during which we were told by our supervisors that we should never discuss or make assignments about anything controversial, such as politics or religion. (I would like to give credit here to all the pioneers and leaders in TESOL—people such as Elsa Auerbach, Sarah Benesch, Suresh Canagarajah, Ryuko Kubota, Angel Lin, Brian Morgan, Bonny Norton, and Alastair Pennycook—who have contributed to making these changes possible, often with some difficulty and controversy.) And of course ESL is situated in the midst of larger historical and sociopolitical/geographic changes: globalization, constantly increasing immigration (including more and more refugees), and the growing (although controversial) worldwide dominance of the English language. We are currently discussing issues that were barely thought of 20 or 30 or 40 years ago in our field, such as student and teacher identities, World Englishes, "linguistic genocide," social and political implications of teaching "survival English," the situations and rights of nonnative English speaker teachers (NNESTs) of English, concerns about mixing religion and English teaching in EFL settings, and more. (For a useful overview of some of the changes, and the current status of our field, see "TESOL's 40th Anniversary Issue" of *TESOL Quarterly* [Canagarajah, 2006].)

Perhaps partly because of these global changes, but also because of the hard work and struggles of many of our predecessors and colleagues, our field has gradually become much more professionalized, with more credentialing, organizations, publications, and conferences, and thus more recognized as a legitimate and valuable discipline in academe. It is still, unfortunately, considered by many to be a "service" field rather than a knowledge-building discipline with academic credibility, but this is changing somewhat, although too slowly. Again, however, this recognition and its rewards are limited to a fairly "elite" few: those who have advanced degrees and have been able to gain full-time tenure track academic positions, with all the privileges that adhere to such positions. As we know, most instructors in ESL, especially in higher education, still work in part-time positions, with inadequate pay, and lack job security, time, funding to do research, and suitable office space. The theme of privilege and its relative scarcity is still a huge factor among instructors in our field.

One aspect of privilege, as it relates to age, is gender. It has been widely noted (e.g., Bernard, 2001), and I can personally corroborate, that middle-aged and older women often feel they have been made invisible. They feel that their talents and contributions are overlooked or denigrated. This is a dangerous waste, harmful for the women themselves as well as for society. As Templer (2003) points out, this invisibility can and does lead to discrimination for aging women, even more than for aging men: "The situation for female TESOLers as they grow older is worsened by a mixture of sexism and ageism that still persists in many locales" (p. 7).

I have suffered some of the ignominy of being treated as inferior because I teach ESL, yet I have also been fortunate enough, after over-coming various obstacles and much uncertainty, to attain a secure, full-time tenured position with the rank of Full Professor, so I have experienced both sides of this coin. (For a description of the changes through the years that I encountered personally, and of related changes through the years in ESL in academe, see Chapter 4.)

As we get older, the ultimate privilege is, of course, good health, closely followed by and connected to good financial health. Once again, those who already have social class privilege are more likely (although obviously not guaranteed) to be healthy, both physically and financially. Those with money and access to good health care are more likely to stay healthy, or to get the best treatment if they become ill. This is as true for educators as for anyone else. But there are differing levels of privi-lege within education; as discussed above, some educators have secure positions with reasonable remuneration and benefits such as subsidized health insurance, but many in our field do not. So the opportunity to grow old in good health, gracefully, and with dignity and joy is not equally allotted, especially in countries such as the United States that lack universal health care. This too is gendered, as women on average live longer than men, and have fewer financial resources during their later years. Growing older is a gift, and often a time when one appreciates more than ever what is truly important in life: family, friends, satisfying work, nature, art, and more. But it is far easier to appreciate these important aspects of life when one has health and enough resources, and it is unfortunate that so many people, including many of our colleagues in TESOL, do not.

I was recently reminded, while rereading a wonderful edited book titled *Wise Women: Reflections of Teachers at Midlife* (Freeman & Schmidt, 2000), of two very positive aspects of teaching in late midlife. First, many academics in late midlife are still driven by, and derive inspiration and energy from, their absolute conviction that (as I summarized their views in my review of the book) "teaching is supremely important, and that teachers make a tremendous contribution. . . . As much as one might believe that . . . years of teaching would wear teachers down and make them cynical, . . . these contributors still see teaching as an almost sacred calling" (Vandrick, 2005, p. 251). Second, the stories in *Wise Women*, and my own experiences and those of other women academics of my age, hearteningly remind us that (again, quoting my review of the book) "life still has many surprises for women at midlife. New events, new challenges, new triumphs still appear and still lie ahead," providing us with a "sense of exhilaration at all the possibilities still ahead" (Vandrick, 2005, p. 251).

Being an older educator is not better or worse than being a young one. What I am reflecting on here is the natural trajectory from new, young teacher to experienced, older teacher, and the different qualities, needs, and feelings experienced at each stage along the way. Our personal lives and teaching lives, so closely connected, grow and evolve through the years, bringing us new strengths and joys as well as new struggles and concerns. As for me, I am still happy to be a teacher and a scholar, and I look forward to the challenges and joys of each stage ahead.

Questions for Reflection
and Discussion

Chapter 1:
An Introduction

1 Do you agree that teachers should take into account their own and their students' backgrounds, identities, and experiences, and their various types of privilege, when teaching, or do you feel that the classroom should be regarded as neutral territory and that teaching should focus only on the material to be covered?

2 Do you feel that teachers' sharing their personal stories in professional venues is useful, or does such sharing seem self-indulgent, or perhaps distracting from the work of education?

3 Is it useful for scholars to experiment with various types of academic writing, and various combinations of those types, or should scholarly writing be only in the form of more traditional academic writing? How does this issue connect with the issue of the various advantages and disadvantages of quantitative vs. qualitative research?

4 Can you think of a time when it was helpful to you to hear a story from another teacher, or from a student, that illuminated an issue for you, or made you feel more connected with colleagues and the field, or helped you to solve a problem you had been dealing with?

Chapter 2:
ESL and the Colonial Legacy:
A Teacher Faces Her "Missionary Kid" Past

1 In which ways do you think our childhood experiences may influence our decisions about teaching? Do you think certain childhood experiences may lead certain people to be drawn to TESOL as a career? How were you personally influenced to choose to teach, and how do your identities and experiences continue to affect the ways you teach and the ways you experience academic life?

2 Do you agree that there is a sort of "colonial legacy" that has influenced, and perhaps still influences, the field of TESOL? If so, how have you seen it manifested in teaching sites and situations that you are familiar with?

Chapter 3:
Tea and TESOL

1 The author focuses on tea as a symbol of her conflicted feelings about her life and teaching: she loves tea, teacups, and other elements of tea drinking, but is also aware of the colonial aspects of teaching that tea evokes. Can you think of other such symbols, perhaps a meaningful object or activity in your own life, that captures your attitudes or conflicts about the teaching life and about being an ESOL teacher?

2 The author sees drinking tea together as a form of community, especially for women. Do you agree? Have you experienced this, or a similar activity, as a type of support and connection with others? What other activities could serve such a purpose? How can such sources of support and connection inform and strengthen us as people and as educators?

Chapter 4:
Shifting Sites, Shifting Identities: A 30-Year Perspective

1 How much do you think our working lives are affected by the sites and situations in which we work?

2 Do you agree that ESOL programs are often marginalized within their larger institutions, and if so, can you give examples from situations you have experienced or are aware of?

3 What can ESOL educators do to improve their working situations? How much is in our individual power to change, and how much requires wider systemic change?

4 The author discussed some aspects of privilege, or lack of privilege, that are evident in ESOL institutional settings; can you think of other aspects of privilege that influence our working lives and the lives of our ESOL students?

Chapter 5:
Fathers and Mentors

1 In what ways can fathers or male mentors influence teachers and the teaching life? Are these different ways from those in which mothers or female mentors influence us?

2 Who have you been most influenced by when going into teaching as a career, and/or as you have progressed during your career? Who has provided you the most, or most useful, mentoring, support, encouragement, and advice?

3 Have you found ways to mentor others in your personal or teaching lives? If so, what have they been?

Chapter 6:
Gender, Class, and the Balanced Life

1 In what ways can it be difficult for female educators and students to balance, or plan to balance, their careers with their family lives?

2 How does social class influence ways in which women and families manage life-work balance dilemmas?

3 How are male educators and students affected by these dilemmas regarding balanced lives? What is their role in addressing them?

4 Which parts of the balance dilemmas can be or should be addressed by individuals, and which parts by larger societal change?

5 What is the role and responsibility of educators to help their students—female and male—to grapple with these issues of work/family balance?

Chapter 7:
Sexual Identity and Education

1 Why do you think that sexual identity issues in education have been so seldom addressed in our professional literature? Is this changing, and if so, why and how? How should it change? What is the obligation of the profession of TESOL, and of professional organizations, toward addressing sexual identity issues?

2 If you have an LGBT identity, what have been your experiences with colleagues and students in your professional and personal lives? Have you been able to be "out" to your colleagues and/or your students?

3 If you are heterosexual, which personal and professional experiences have shaped your knowledge and feelings about sexual identity, and especially sexual identity and education? Do you try to be aware that any of your colleagues or students could have minority sexual identities? How have you responded to LGBT students and colleagues?

4 As an educator, and particularly as an ESOL educator, whether you are LGBT or heterosexual, how do you handle sexual identity issues in your classes? Do you specifically address them, perhaps through statements of respect for all identities, or through materials or curricula? How do you handle homophobic remarks or jokes in class, or in faculty offices?

5 What kinds of information and discussion of sexual identity issues would you like to see in teacher education programs, and in our professional literature and at our professional conferences? Try to think of specific information, or specific formats or venues of discussion, that would be most helpful to you.

Chapter 8:
On Beginning to Write at 40

1 Which types of privilege allow some educators, but not others, to lead a scholarly life and do scholarly research and writing? How can institutions and organizations provide assistance and conditions that encourage more educators to do research and write, if they would like to?

2 Do you think female and male scholars have different issues to deal with in regards to their research and writing? If so, what are those differences?

3 What have been your own experiences, if any, in doing research and writing as a second language or ESOL educator? If you could change certain things to allow you to write more, and be more supported in your writing, what would those things be?

Chapter 9:
The Power of Writing Groups

1 What do you see as the advantages of participating in writing groups? Disadvantages?

2 Have you ever participated in a writing group, or writing retreat, or related group or activity? Was it helpful to you, and if so, how?

3 If you believe that writing groups could be useful to you and your colleagues, what specific steps could you take to initiate such groups? Who could you speak with? What requests and/ or arrangements could you make?

Chapter 10:
The Aging Educator

1 What differences do you see in the ways younger and older educators teach? Is it possible to make generalizations, or are differences purely individual and unrelated to age? If there are differences, what are the strengths and weaknesses of each age?

2 Have you seen yourself changing your teaching styles, and your attitudes about teaching, as you have gotten older, or do you predict that you will change in the future? What kinds of things have you learned as you have gotten older, and/or do you think you will learn as you get older?

3 Have you ever experienced, or seen, prejudice or discrimination against faculty or students because of their age, whether young or old? What happened? What could be done, or could have been done, to prevent or address that discrimination?

4 What can individuals and institutions do to ensure that educators feel supported at all stages of their careers, and remain active and engaged throughout those careers?

References

Achebe, C. (1994). Dead man's path. In R. Spack (Ed.), *The international short story: An anthology with guidelines for reading and writing about fiction* (pp. 113–115). New York: St. Martin's Press. (Original work published 1953)

Anderson et al. (1997, August/September). [Letter to the editor]. *TESOL Matters, 7*(4), 22.

Apter, T. (1993). *Working women don't have wives: Professional success in the 1990's.* New York: St. Martin's Press.

Auerbach, E. R. (1991). Politics, pedagogy, and professionalism: Challenging marginalization in ESL. *College ESL, 1*(1), 1–9.

———. (1993). Putting the P back in participatory. *TESOL Quarterly, 27*(3), 543–545.

Auerbach, E. R., & Burgess, D. (1985). The hidden curriculum of survival ESL. *TESOL Quarterly, 19*(3), 475–495.

Austen, J. (1957). *Emma* (L. Trilling, Ed.). Boston: Houghton Mifflin. (Original work published 1816)

———. (1964). *Mansfield Park.* New York: Signet. (Original work published 1814)

Azar, B. S. (1999). *Understanding and using English grammar* (3rd ed.). Upper Saddle River, NJ: Prentice Hall Regents.

Balif, M., Davis, D. D., & Mountford, R. (2008). *Women's ways of making it in rhetoric and composition.* New York: Routledge.

Barnard, I. (n.d.). Anti-homophobic pedagogy: Some suggestions for teachers. *Radical Teacher, 45,* 26–28.

Bateson, M. C. (1994). *Peripheral visions.* New York: HarperCollins.

Behar, R. (1993). *Translated woman: Crossing the border with Esperanza's story.* Boston: Beacon.

Belcher, D., & Connor, U. (Eds.). (2001). *Reflections on multiliterate lives.* Clevedon, UK: Multilingual Matters.

Belkin, L. (2003, October 26). The opt-out revolution. *New York Times Magazine,* p. 42.

Bell, J. S. (2002). Narrative inquiry: More than just telling stories. *TESOL Quarterly, 36*(2), 207–213.

Bellah, R. N., Madsen, R., Sullivan, W. M., Swidler, A., & Tipton, S. M. (1985). *Habits of the heart*. New York: Harper & Row.

Benesch, S. (Ed.). (1988). *Ending remediation: Linking ESL and content in higher education*. Alexandria, VA: TESOL.

———. (1991). ESL on campus: Questioning testing and tracking policies. In S. Benesch (Ed.), *ESL in America: Myths and possibilities* (pp. 59–74). Portsmouth, NH: Boynton/Cook/Heinemann.

———. (2001). *Critical English for academic purposes: Theory, politics, and practice*. Mahwah, NJ: Lawrence Erlbaum.

Bernard, M. (2001). Women ageing: Old lives, new challenges. *Education and Ageing, 16*(3), 333–352.

Bishop, W. (1997). *Teaching lives: Essays and stories*. Logan: Utah State University Press.

Blanton, L. L. (2002). As I was saying to Leonard Bloomfield: A personalized history of ESL/writing. In L. L. Blanton & B. Kroll, *ESL composition tales: Reflections on teaching* (pp. 135–162). Ann Arbor: University of Michigan Press.

Blanton, L. L., & Kroll, B. (2002). *ESL composition tales: Reflections on teaching*. Ann Arbor: University of Michigan Press.

Bloom, L. Z. (1992). Teaching college English as a woman. *College English, 54*(7), 818–825.

———. (1996). Freshman composition as a middle-class enterprise. *College English, 58*(6), 654–675.

Bourdieu, P., & Passeron, J.-C. (1977). *Reproduction in education, society and culture* (R. Nice & T. Bottommore, Trans.). London: Sage.

Braine, G. (Ed.). (1999). *Non-native educators in English language teaching*. Mahwah, NJ: Lawrence Erlbaum.

Britzman, D. P. (1995). Is there a queer pedagogy? Or, stop reading straight. *Educational Theory, 45*(2), 151–165.

———. (1998). Queer pedagogy and its strange techniques. In J. L. Ristock & C. G. Taylor (Eds.), *Inside the academy and out: Lesbian/gay/queer studies and social action* (pp. 49–71). Toronto: University of Toronto Press.

Bruner, J. (1991). The narrative construction of reality. *Critical Inquiry, 18*(1), 1–21.

Burdell, P., & Swadener, B. B. (1999). Critical personal narrative and autoethnography in education: Reflections on a genre. *Educational Researcher, 28*(6), 21–26.

Canagarajah, A. S. (1993). Critical ethnography of a Sri Lankan classroom: Ambiguities in student opposition to reproduction through ESOL. *TESOL Quarterly, 27*(4), 601–626.

————. (2002). *Critical academic writing and multilingual students.* Ann Arbor: University of Michigan Press.

————. (Ed.). (2006). TESOL's 40th anniversary issue [Special issue]. *TESOL Quarterly, 40*(1).

Casanave, C. P., & Schecter, S. R. (Eds.). (1997). *On becoming a language educator: Personal essays on professional development.* Mahwah, NJ: Lawrence Erlbaum.

Casanave, C. P., & Sosa, M. (2007). *Respite for teachers: Reflection and renewal in the teaching life.* Ann Arbor: University of Michigan Press.

Casanave, C. P., & Vandrick, S. (2003a). Introduction: Issues in writing for publication. In C. P. Casanave & S. Vandrick (Eds.), *Writing for scholarly publication: Behind the scenes in language education* (pp. 1–13). Mahwah, NJ: Lawrence Erlbaum.

————. (Eds.). (2003b). *Writing for scholarly publication: Behind the scenes in language education.* Mahwah, NJ: Lawrence Erlbaum.

Chatterjee, P. (2001). *A time for tea: Women, labor, and postcolonial politics on an Indian plantation.* Durham, NC: Duke University Press.

Clandinin, D. J., & Connelly, F. M. (2000). *Narrative inquiry: Experience and story in qualitative research.* San Francisco: Jossey-Bass.

Clarke, M. A. (2003). *A place to stand: Essays for educators in troubled times.* Ann Arbor: University of Michigan Press.

————. (2007). *Common ground, contested territory: Examining the roles of English language teachers in troubled times.* Ann Arbor: University of Michigan Press.

Coiner, C., Frankenstein, M., Miller, J. A., Rudnick, L. P., & Slapikoff, S. (1995). Class in the classroom: Transcription of an American Studies Association workshop. *Radical Teacher, 46,* 46–48.

Coles, R. (1989). *The call of stories: Teaching and the moral imagination.* Boston: Houghton Mifflin.

Connelly, F. M., & Clandinin, D. J. (Eds.). (1999). *Shaping a professional identity: Stories of education practice.* New York: Teachers College Press.

Cummins, H. A. (2005). Mommy tracking single women in academia when they are not mommies. *Women's Studies International Forum, 28*(2–3), 222–231.

Curran, G. (2006). Responding to students' normative questions about gays: Putting queer theory into practice in an Australian ESL class. *Journal of Language, Identity, and Education, 5*(1), 85–96.

Curtis, A., & Romney, M. (Eds.) (2006). *Color, race, and English language teaching: Shades of meaning.* Mahwah, NJ: Lawrence Erlbaum.

Czarniawska, B. (2004). *Narratives in social science research.* Thousand Oaks, CA: Sage.

Daiute, C., & Lightfoot, C. (Eds.). (2004). *Narrative analysis: Studying the development of individuals in society.* Thousand Oaks, CA: Sage.

Davis, K. A., & Skilton-Sylvester, E. (Eds.). (2004). Gender and languge education. [Special issue]. *TESOL Quarterly, 38*(3).

De, E. N., & Gregory, D. U. (1997). Decolonizing the classroom: Freshman composition in a multicultural setting. In C. Severino, J. C. Guerra, & J. E. Butler (Eds.), *Writing in multicultural settings* (pp. 118–132). New York: Modern Language Association.

de Albuquerque, K. (1998). On golliwogs and flit pumps: How the Empire stays with us in strange remembrances. *Jouvert: A Journal of Postcolonial Studies, 2*(2), n.p. Retrieved May 22, 2009, from http://english.chass.ncsu.edu/jouvert/v2i2/KLAUSAL.HTM

Dean, A. V. (1998). Teaching and writing "As if [my] life depended on it." In J. Z. Schmidt (Ed.), *Women/Writing/Teaching* (pp. 119–132). Albany: State University of New York Press.

DeGenaro, W. (2001). Class consciousness and the junior college movement: Creating a docile workforce. *JAC, 21*(3), 499–520.

Densmore, D. (n.d.). *Sex roles and female oppression.* [Pamphlet]. Boston: New England Free Press.

Denzin, N. K., & Lincoln, Y. S. (2002). Editors' introduction. In N. K. Denzin & Y. S. Lincoln (Eds.), *The qualitative inquiry reader* (pp. ix–xvi). Thousand Oaks, CA: Sage.

Dews, C. L. B., & Law, C. L. (Eds.). (1995). *This fine place so far from home: Voices of academics from the working class.* Philadelphia: Temple University Press.

———. (1998). Anti-intellectualism, homophobia, and the working-class gay/lesbian academic. *Radical Teacher, 53,* 8–12.

Didion, J. (2005). *The year of magical thinking.* New York: Knopf.

Dunbar, R. (n.d.). *Female liberation as the basis for social revolution.* [Pamphlet]. Boston: New England Free Press.

Ellis, C. (1997). Evocative autoethnography: Writing emotionally about our lives. In W. G. Tierney & Y. S. Lincoln (Eds.), *Representation and the text: Re-framing the narrative voice* (pp. 115–139). Carbondale: Southern Illinois University Press.

Evans, E., & Grant, C. (Eds.). (2008). *Mama, PhD: Women write about motherhood and academic life.* New Brunswick, NJ: Rutgers University Press.

Field, N. (1995). *Over the rainbow: Money, class, and homophobia.* London: Pluto Press.

Fine, M., Weis, L., Weseen, S., & Wong, L. (2000). For whom? Qualitative research, representations, and social responsibilities. In N. K. Denzin & Y. S. Lincoln (Eds.), *Handbook of qualitative research* (2nd ed., pp. 107–131). Thousand Oaks, CA: Sage.

Folse, K. (1996). *Discussion starters: Speaking fluency activities for advanced ESL/EFL students.* Ann Arbor: University of Michigan Press.

Fontaine, S. I., & Hunter, S. (Eds.). (1993). *Writing ourselves into the story: Unheard voices from composition studies.* Carbondale: Southern Illinois University Press.

Ford, F. (1997). Worthwhile causes and educator responsibility [Letter to the editor]. *TESOL Matters, 7*(5), 6.

Forster, E. M. (1952). *A passage to India.* New York: Harcourt, Brace and World. (Original work published 1924)

Fox, H. (1994). *Listening to the world: Cultural issues in academic writing.* Urbana, IL: National Council of Teachers of English.

Franeta, S. (2001). Merging life and language teaching. *Journal of Engaged Pedagogy, 1*(1), 48–64.

Freedman, D. P., & Frey, O. (Eds.). (2003). *Autobiographical writing across the disciplines: A reader.* Durham, NC: Duke University Press.

Freeman, P. R., & Schmidt, J. Z. (Eds.). (2000). *Wise women: Reflections of teachers at midlife.* New York: Routledge.

Gebhardt, R. (Ed.). (1992). Personal and innovative writing [Special issue]. *College Composition and Communication, 43*(1).

Geertz, C. (1995). *After the fact: Two countries, four decades, one anthropologist.* Cambridge, MA: Harvard University Press.

Goodwin, L. D., Stevens, E. A., & Bellamy, G. T. (1998). Mentoring among faculty in schools, colleges and departments of education. *Journal of Teacher Education, 49*(5), 334–343.

Hadley, T. (2007). *The master bedroom.* New York: Holt.

Hafernik, J. J., Messerschmitt, D. S., & Vandrick, S. (1997). Collaborative research: Why and how. *Educational Researcher, 26*(9), 31–35.

———. (2002). *Ethical issues for ESL faculty: Social justice in practice.* Mahwah, NJ: Lawrence Erlbaum.

Hall, J., Mueller, I., & Stahl, B. (2003). *How does a writing circle help faculty members?* Retrieved May 23, 2009, from www.msvu.ca/tlc/WIC/MR_1_1_Hall_Mueller,_Stahl.pdf

Hampl, P. (1999). *I could tell you stories: Sojourns in the land of memory.* New York: Norton.

———. (2007). *The florist's daughter.* New York: Harcourt.

Hancock, E. (1989). *The girl within: A groundbreaking new approach to female identity.* New York: Fawcett Columbine.

Haroian-Guerin, G. (Ed.). (1999). *The personal narrative: Writing ourselves as teachers and scholars.* Portland, ME: Calendar Islands.

Hart, E. L. (with Parmeter, S.-H.). (1992). 'Writing in the margins': A lesbian- and gay-inclusive course. In C. M. Hurlbert & S. Totten (Eds.), *Social issues in the English classroom* (pp. 154–173). Urbana, IL: National Council of Teachers of English.

Hedgcock, J. (2003). Reflections on coauthorship and the professional dialogue: Risks and rewards. In C. P. Casanave & S. Vandrick (Eds.), *Writing for scholarly publication: Behind the scenes in language education* (pp. 113–127). Mahwah, NJ: Lawrence Erlbaum.

Heilbrun, C. G. (1988). *Writing a woman's life.* New York: Norton.

Hemmert, A., & Kappra, R. (2004). *Out and about: An interactive course in beginning English.* San Francisco: Alta Book Publishers.

Herron, J. (1992). Writing for my father. *College English, 54*(8), 928–937.

Hesford, W. S. (1997). Writing identities: The essence of difference in multicultural classrooms. In C. Severino, J. C. Guerra, & J. E. Butler (Eds.), *Writing in multicultural settings* (pp. 133–149). New York: Modern Language Association.

Hindman, J. E. (Ed.). (2001). Personal writing [Special focus]. *College English, 64*(1).

———. (Ed.). (2003). The personal in academic writing [Special issue]. *College English, 66*(1).

Hochschild, A. R. (1997). *The time bind: When work becomes home and home becomes work.* New York: Metropolitan.

hooks, b. (2000a, November 17). Learning in the shadow of race and class [Electronic version]. *Chronicle of Higher Education, 47*(12), B14–16.

———. (2000b). *Where we stand: Class matters.* New York: Routledge.

Imamura, S. (2001). *Shig: The true story of an American kamikaze.* Baltimore: American Literary Press.

James, H. (1983). *The portrait of a lady.* New York: Modern Library. (Original work published 1881)

Janopoulos, M. (1992). University faculty tolerance of NS and NNS writing errors: A comparison. *Journal of Second Language Writing, 1*(2), 109–121.

Jarvis, D. K. (1991). *Junior faculty development: A handbook.* New York: Modern Language Association.

Jewell, J. B. W. (1998). A transgendered ESL learner in relation to her class textbooks, heterosexist hegemony and change. *Melbourne Papers in Applied Linguistics, 10*, 1–21.

Johnson, K. E., & Golombek, P. R. (Eds.). (2002). *Narrative inquiry as professional development.* New York: Cambridge University Press.

Johnston, L. (2008, March 17). For better or worse. *San Francisco Chronicle*, p. E6.

Kachru, B. B. (1993). *The other tongue: English across cultures* (2nd ed.). Urbana: University of Illinois Press.

Kaplan, A. (1993). *French lessons: A memoir.* Chicago: University of Chicago Press.

Kappra, R. (1998/1999, December/January). Addressing heterosexism in the IEP classroom. *TESOL Matters, 8*(6), 19.

————. (1999, February). Who gets excluded from your lesson? *CATESOL News*, *30*(4), 3–4.

Kappra, R., & Vandrick, S. (2006) Silenced voices: Queer ESL students recount their experiences. *CATESOL Journal*, *18*(1), 138–150.

Kindlon, D. (2006). *Alpha girls: Understanding the new American girl and how she is changing the world.* New York: Rodale.

Klinkenborg, V. (2008, January 4). Life, love and the pleasures of literature in Barsetshire. *New York Times*, p. A18.

Kouritzin, S. G. (2004). The British Columbia literature 12 curriculum and I: A soliloquy. *Curriculum Inquiry*, *34*(2), 185–212.

Kubota, R. (2003). New approaches to gender, class, and race in second language writing. *Journal of Second Language Writing*, *12*(1), 31–47.

Kuwahara, K. K. (2004). Jane Austen's Emma and empire: A postcolonial view. *Persuasions On-Line*, *25*(1). Retrieved May 22, 2009, from www.jasna.org/persuasions/on-line/vol25no1/kuwahara.html

Leki, I. (1997). Cross-talk: ESL issues and contrastive rhetoric. In C. Severino, J. C. Guerra, & J. E. Butler (Eds.), *Writing in multicultural settings* (pp. 234–244). New York: Modern Language Association.

————. (2002). Not the end of history. In L. L. Blanton & B. Kroll, *ESL composition tales: Reflections on teaching* (pp. 49–62). Ann Arbor: University of Michigan Press.

Lessing, D. (2007, December 7). *On not winning the Nobel Prize.* Speech presented at the Nobel Prize ceremony, Stockholm, Sweden. Retrieved December 11, 2007, from http://nobelprize.org/nobel_prizes/literature/laureates/2007/lessing-lecture_en.html

Li, G., & Beckett, G. H. (Eds.). (2006). *"Strangers" of the academy: Asian women scholars in higher education.* Sterling, VA: Stylus.

Lim, S. G.-l. (1996). *Among the white moon faces: An Asian-American memoir of homelands.* New York: Feminist Press.

Lin, A., Grant, R., Kubota, R., Motha, S., Tinker Sachs, G., Vandrick, S., & Wong, S. (2004). Women faculty of color in TESOL: Theorizing our lived experiences. *TESOL Quarterly*, *38*(3), 487–504.

Lindstromberg, S. (1997, June/July). A call for balance [Letter to the editor]. *TESOL Matters*, *7*(3), 21.

Littell, F. H. (1997). First they came for the Jews [Electronic version]. *Christian Ethics Today: Journal of Christian Ethics*, *3*(1).

Lubetsky, M. H. (1998). 'Sensei, I slashed my wrists last night.' *The Language Teacher*, *22*(5), 44–45.

Matsuda, P. K. (1998). Situating ESL writing in a cross-disciplinary context. *Written Communication, 15*(1), 99–121.

———. (1999). Composition studies and ESL writing: A disciplinary division of labor. *College Composition and Communication, 50*(4), 699–721.

———. (2003). Second language writing in the twentieth century: A situated historical perspective. In B. Kroll (Ed.), *Exploring the dynamics of second language writing* (pp. 15–34). New York: Cambridge University Press.

McCracken, H. T., & Larson, R. L. (with J. Entes). (Eds.). (1998). *Teaching college English and English education: Reflective stories.* Urbana, IL: National Council of Teachers of English.

McIntosh, P. (1988). *White privilege and male privilege: A personal account of coming to see correspondences through work in Women's Studies.* Working paper no. 189. Wellesley, MA: Wellesley College, Center for Research on Women.

Merisotis, J. P., & Phipps, R. A. (2000). Remedial education in colleges and universities: What's really going on? *The Review of Higher Education, 24*(1), 67–85.

Miller, A. (1999). *Death of a salesman.* New York: Penguin. (Original work published 1949)

Miller, N. K. (1991). *Getting personal: Feminist occasions and other autobiographical acts.* New York: Routledge.

———. (1997). Public statements, private lives: Academic memoirs for the nineties. *Signs, 22*(4), 981–1015.

———. (2002). *But enough about me: Why we read other people's lives.* New York: Columbia University Press.

Moita-Lopes, L. P. (2006). Queering literacy teaching: Analyzing gay-themed discourses in a fifth-grade class in Brazil. *Journal of Language, Identity, and Education, 5*(1), 31–50.

Morgan, B. D. (1998). *The ESL classroom: Teaching, critical practice, and community development.* Toronto: University of Toronto Press.

Motha, S. (2006). Racializing ESOL teacher identities in U.S. K–12 public schools. *TESOL Quarterly, 40*(3), 495–518.

Murray, M. (1991). *Beyond the myths and magic of mentoring: How to facilitate an effective mentoring program.* San Francisco: Jossey-Bass.

Musil, C. M. (2007, Fall). Scaling the ivory towers. *Ms., 17*(4), 43–45.

Nash, R. J. (2004). *Liberating scholarly writing: The power of personal narrative.* New York: Teachers College Press.

National Research Council of the National Academies. (2007). *To recruit and advance: Women students and faculty in science and engineering.* Washington, DC: National Academies Press.

Nelson, C. (1993). Heterosexism in ESL: Examining our attitudes. *TESOL Quarterly, 27*(1), 143–150.

————. (1999). Sexual identities in ESL: Queer theory and classroom inquiry. *TESOL Quarterly, 33*(3), 371–391.

————. (2002, March). *"Queer as a second language": Classroom theater for everyone.* Spotlight session presented at the annual meeting of TESOL, Salt Lake City, UT.

————. (2004). Beyond straight grammar: Using lesbian/gay themes to explore cultural meanings. In B. Norton & A. Pavlenko (Eds.), *Gender and English language learners* (pp. 15–28). Alexandria, VA: TESOL.

————. (2005). Transnational/queer: Narratives from the contact zone. *Journal of Curriculum Theorizing, 21*(2), 109–117.

————. (Ed.). (2006a). Queer inquiry in language education [Special issue]. *Journal of Language, Identity, and Education, 5*(1).

————. (2006b). Queer inquiry in language education. *Journal of Language, Identity, and Education, 5*(1), 1–9.

————. (2009). *Sexual identities in English language education: Classroom conversations.* New York: Routledge.

Nguyen, H. T., & Kellogg, G. (2005). Emergent identities in on-line discussions for second language learning [Electronic version]. *The Canadian Modern Language Review, 62*(1), 111–136.

Norton, B. (2000). *Identity and language learning: Gender, ethnicity and educational change.* New York: Longman/Pearson.

Norton, B., & Pavlenko, A. (Eds.). (2004). *Gender and English language learners.* Alexandria, VA: TESOL.

O'Dair, S. (2003). Class work: Site of egalitarian activism or site of embourgeoisement? *College English, 65*(6), 593–606.

Ohmann, R. (2003). Is class an identity? *Radical Teacher, 68,* 10–12.

O'Mochain, R., Mitchell, M., & Nelson, C. (2003). Dialogues around "Heterosexism in ESL: Examining our attitudes" and "Sexual identities in ESL: Queer theory and classroom inquiry" (1993, 1999). In J. Sharkey & K. E. Johnson (Eds.), *The TESOL Quarterly dialogues: Rethinking issues of language, culture, and power* (pp. 123–140). Alexandria, VA: TESOL.

O'Neill, J. (2008). *Netherland.* New York: Pantheon.

Pavlenko, A. (2001). "How am I to become a woman in an American vein?": Transformations of gender performance in second language learning. In A. Pavlenko, A. Blackledge, I. Piller, & M. Teutsch-Dwyer (Eds.), *Multilingualism, second language learning, and gender* (pp. 133–174). New York: Mouton de Gruyter.

————. (2002). Narrative study: Whose story is it, anyway? *TESOL Quarterly, 36*(2), 213–218.

————. (2007). Autobiographical narratives as data in applied linguistics. *Applied Linguistics, 28*(2), 163–188.

Pavlenko, A., Blackledge, A., Piller, I., & Teutsch-Dwyer, M. (Eds.). (2001). *Multilingualism, second language learning, and gender.* New York: Mouton de Gruyter.

Pennycook, A. (2001). *Critical applied linguistics: A critical introduction.* Mahwah, NJ: Lawrence Erlbaum.

Phillion, J. (2005). Narrative in teacher education. In P. C. Miller (Ed.), *Narratives from the classroom: An introduction to teaching* (pp. 1–11). Thousand Oaks, CA: Sage.

Phillipson, R. (1992). *Linguistic imperialism.* New York: Oxford University Press.

Pipher, M. B. (1995). *Reviving Ophelia: Saving the selves of adolescent girls.* New York: Putnam.

Plath, S. (1966). Daddy. In *Ariel* (pp. 49–51). New York: Harper and Row.

Polkinghorne, D. E. (1988). *Narrative knowing and the human sciences.* Albany: State University of New York Press.

Porter, E. (2006, March 2). Women in workplace—trend is reversing. *San Francisco Chronicle*, p. A2.

Proweller, A. (1998). *Constructing female identities: Meaning making in an upper middle class youth culture.* Albany: State University of New York Press.

Raffo, S. (Ed.). (1997). *Queerly classed.* Boston: South End.

Reed, E. (n.d.). *The myth of women's inferiority.* [Pamphlet]. Boston: New England Free Press.

Renner, C. E. (1998). Looking at publishers' attitudes. *TESOL Matters, 7*(6), 15.

Richardson, L. (1997). *Fields of play: Constructing an academic life.* New Brunswick, NJ: Rutgers University Press.

Ritchie, J. S., & Wilson, D. E. (2000). *Teacher narrative as critical inquiry: Rewriting the script.* New York: Teachers College Press.

Roen, D. H., Brown, S. C., & Enos, T. (Eds.). (1999). *Living rhetoric and composition: Stories of the discipline.* Mahwah, NJ: Lawrence Erlbaum.

Rose, M. (1985). The language of exclusion: Writing instruction at the university. *College English, 47*(4), 341–359.

Rubin, L. (1979). *Women of a certain age: The midlife search for self.* New York: Harper and Row.

Schenke, A. (1991). The "will to reciprocity" and the work of memory: Fictioning speaking out of silence in E.S.L. and feminist pedagogy. *Resources for Feminist Research, 20*, 47–55.

————. (1996). Not just a "social issue": Teaching feminist in ESL. *TESOL Quarterly, 30*, 155–159.

Schinto, J. (1997, October 13). Lessing in London [Review of the book *Walking in the shade: Volume two of my autobiography, 1949–1962*]. *The Nation, 275*, 31–33.

Schmidt, J. Z. (Ed.). (1998). *Women/writing/teaching*. Albany: State University of New York Press.

Schoenfeld, C., & Magnan, R. (1994). *Mentor in a manual: Climbing the academic ladder to tenure*. Madison, WI: Magna.

Sebold, A. (2007). *The almost moon*. New York: Little, Brown.

Shafiei, M. (1997, August/September). Treating IEP students as knowledgeable adults (Part 1). *TESOL Matters, 7*(4), 10.

Shakespeare, W. (2005). *The tragedy of King Lear* (J. L. Halio, Ed.). New York: Cambridge University Press. (Original work published 1623)

Sharkey, J. (2004). Lives stories don't tell: Exploring the untold in autobiographies. *Curriculum Inquiry, 34*(4), 495–512.

Shen, F. (1989). The classroom and the wider culture: Identity as a key to learning English composition. *College Composition and Communication, 40*(4), 456–459.

Shepard, A., McMillan, J., & Tate, G. (Eds.). (1998). *Coming to class: Pedagogy and the social class of teachers*. Westport, CT: Heinemann/Boynton/Cook.

Sisterhood and the small group. (n.d.). [Broadsheet, no publisher].

Smiley, J. (1991). *A thousand acres*. New York: Knopf.

Snelbecker, K. (1994). *Speaking out: A survey of lesbian, gay, and bisexual teachers of ESOL in the U. S.* Unpublished master's thesis, School for International Training, Brattleboro, VT. (ERIC Document Reproduction Service No. FL022537)

Snelbecker, K., & Meyer, T. (1996, August/September). Dealing with sexual orientation in the classroom. *TESOL Matters, 6*(4), 19.

Soliday, M. (1999). Class dismissed. *College English, 61*(6), 731–741.

———. (2002). *The politics of remediation: Institutional and student needs in higher education*. Pittsburgh, PA: University of Pittsburgh Press.

Sommers, N. (1992). Between the drafts. *College Composition and Communication, 43*(1), 23–31.

———. (1993). I stand here writing. *College English, 55*(4), 420–428.

———. (1998). The language of coats. *College English, 60*(4), 421–425.

Southam, B. (1995, February 17). The silence of the Bertrams: Slavery and the chronology of *Mansfield Park*. *Times Literary Supplement*, pp. 13–14.

Spack, R. (1997). The (in)visibility of the person(al) in academe. *College English, 59*(1), 9–31.

Spigelman, C. (2004). *Personally speaking: Experience as evidence in academic discourse.* Carbondale: Southern Illinois University Press.

St. Aubyn, E. (2003). *Some hope: A trilogy.* New York: Open City.

Staying at home [Television series episode]. (2005, July 17). In *Sixty Minutes.* Retrieved February 6, 2009, from www.cbsnews.com/stories/2005/07/11/60minutes/main 708196.shtml

Sternglass, M. (1997). *Time to know them.* Mahwah, NJ: Lawrence Erlbaum.

Sullivan, P. A. (1998). Passing: A family dissemblance. In A. Shepard, J. McMillan, & G. Tate (Eds.), *Coming to class: Pedagogy and the social class of teachers* (pp. 231–251). Portsmouth, NH: Boynton/Cook/Heinemann.

Summerhawk, B. (1998). From closet to classroom: Gay issues in ESL/EFL. *The Language Teacher, 22*(5), 21–23.

Tate, G. (1997). Thinking about our class. *Journal of Basic Writing, 16*(1), 13–17.

Templer, B. (2003). Ageism in TEFL: Time for concerted action. *TESL Reporter, 36*(1), 1–22.

Tharenou, P. (1994). Why so few female senior academics? *Australian Journal of Management, 19*(2), 221–228.

Thewlis, S. H. (1997). *Grammar dimensions: Book three* (2nd ed.). Boston: Heinle & Heinle.

Tierney, W. G. (1997). *Academic outlaws: Queer theory and cultural studies in the academy.* Thousand Oaks, CA: Sage.

Tierney, W. G., & Lincoln, Y. S. (Eds.). (1997). *Representation and the text: Re-framing the narrative voice.* Albany: State University of New York Press.

Tokarczyk, M. M., & Fay, E. A. (Eds.). (1993). *Working-class women in the academy: Laborers in the knowledge factory.* Amherst: University of Massachusetts Press.

Tollefson, J. W. (1991). *Planning language, planning inequality: Language policy in the community.* London: Longman.

———. (Ed.). (1995). *Power and inequality in language education.* New York: Cambridge University Press.

Tompkins, J. (1987). Me and my shadow. *New Literary History, 19*(1), 169–178.

———. (1990). Pedagogy of the distressed. *College English, 52*(6), 653–660.

———. (1996). *A life in school: What the teacher learned.* New York: Addison-Wesley.

Toth, E. (1997). *Ms. Mentor's impeccable advice for women in academia.* Philadelphia: University of Pennsylvania Press.

Trimmer, J. (Ed.). (1997). *Narration as knowledge: Tales of the teaching life.* Portsmouth, NH: Boynton/Cook.

University of San Francisco General Catalog. (2005–2007).

University of Southern California Center for Excellence in Teaching. (2003). *Faculty mentoring paper summary: Mellon academic mentoring support project.* Retrieved November 30, 2007, from www.usc.edu/programs/cet/private/pdfs/mentor/facultypaper.pdf

Vandrick, S. (1992). Politics in the university ESL class. *CATESOL Journal, 5*(2), 19–27.

———. (1993). Feminist fiction for social change. *Peace Review, 5,* 507–510.

———. (1994a). Feminist pedagogy and ESL. *College ESL, 4*(2), 69–92.

———. (1994b). Teaching social justice issues through literature. *CATESOL Journal, 7*(2), 113–119.

———. (1995a). Privileged ESL university students. *TESOL Quarterly, 29*(2), 375–381.

———. (1995b). Teaching and practicing feminism in the university ESL class. *TESOL Journal, 4*(3), 4–6.

———. (1996). Issues in using multicultural literature in college ESL classes. *Journal of Second Language Writing, 5*(3), 253–269.

———. (1997a). Diaspora literature: A mirror for ESL students. *College ESL, 7*(2), 53–69.

———. (1997b, April/May). Heterosexual teachers' part in fighting homophobia. *TESOL Matters, 7*(2), 23.

———. (1997c). Reading and responding to novels in the university ESL classroom. *The Journal of the Imagination in Language Learning, 4,* 104–107.

———. (1997d, October/November). Response [to Frank Ford's letter] [Letter to the editor]. *TESOL Matters, 7*(5), 6.

———. (1997e). The role of hidden identities in the postsecondary ESL classroom. *TESOL Quarterly, 31*(1), 153–157.

———. (1998). Promoting gender equity in the postsecondary ESL class. In T. Smoke (Ed.), *Adult ESL: Politics, pedagogy, and participation in classroom and community programs* (pp. 73–88). Mahwah, NJ: Lawrence Erlbaum.

———. (1999a, April/May). The case for more research on female students in the ESL/EFL classroom. *TESOL Matters, 9*(2), 16.

———. (1999b). A school parent group which supports families, education, and community. *Education, 120*(2), 249–253.

———. (1999c, February/March). Who's afraid of critical feminist pedagogies? *TESOL Matters, 9*(1), 9.

———. (2001a). Teachers' cultures, teachers' stories. *Journal of Engaged Pedagogy, 1,* 19–39.

———. (2001b). *Teaching sexual identity issues in university ESL classes.* Paper presented at the annual meeting of TESOL, St. Louis. (ERIC Document Reproduction Service No. 474 464).

————. (2003). Literature in the teaching of L2 composition. In B. Kroll (Ed.), *Exploring the dynamics of second language writing* (pp. 263–283). New York: Cambridge University Press.

————. (2004). A comparative review of four books on language and gender [Review of the books *Gender in the language classroom, Language and gender, Gender identity and discourse analysis,* and *Communicating gender*]. *TESOL Quarterly, 38*(3), 539–544.

————. (2005). [Review of the book *Wise women: Reflections of teachers at midlife*]. *Feminist Teacher, 15*(3), 250–251.

————. (2007, April). *Understanding students of the new global elite.* Paper presented at the meeting of the International Society for Language Studies, Honolulu, HI.

————. (2008a, April). *Sexual identity and social class.* Paper presented at the meeting of CATESOL, Sacramento, CA.

————. (2008b, April). *Stories from queer ESOL students.* Paper presented at the meeting of TESOL, New York.

————. (in press). Social class privilege among ESOL writing students. In M. Cox, J. Jordan, G. G. Schwartz, & C. Ortmeier-Hooper (Eds.), *Reinventing identities in second language writing.* Urbana, IL: National Council of Teachers of English.

Wallis, C. (2004, March 22). The case for staying home [Electronic version]. *Time,* 50–59.

Walsh, J. (2006, February 6). Feminism after Friedan. *Salon.com.* Retrieved February 6, 2009, from salon.com/mwt/feature/2006/02/06/friedan

White, G. D. V. (2006). *Jane Austen in the context of abolition: 'A fling at the slave trade.'* New York: Palgrave Macmillan.

Wildman, S. M. (1996). *Privilege revealed: How invisible preference undermines America.* New York: New York University Press.

Willard-Traub, M. K. (2006). Reflection in academe: Scholarly writing and the shifting subject. *College English, 68*(4), 422–432.

Williams, J. (1995). ESL program administration in the United States. *Journal of Second Language Writing, 4*(2), 157–179.

Williams, P. (1991). *The alchemy of race and rights: Diary of a law professor.* Cambridge, MA: Harvard University Press.

Witherell, C., & Noddings, N. (Eds.). (1991). *Stories lives tell: Narrative and dialogue in education.* New York: Teachers College Press.

Woo, C. (1999). Incarnating an Asian American angel: 'Self-expression', ontology, and pedagogy. In G. Haroian-Guerin (Ed.), *The personal narrative: Writing ourselves as teachers and scholars* (pp. 75–87). Portland, ME: Calendar Islands.

Woolf, V. (1959). *A room of one's own.* London: Hogarth Press. (Original work published 1929)

Zamel, V. (1995). Strangers in academia: The experiences of faculty and ESL students across the curriculum. *College Composition and Communication, 46*(4), 506–521.

————. (1996). Transcending boundaries: Complicating the scene of teaching language. *College ESL, 6*(2), 1–11.

Zandy, J. (Ed.). (1994). *Liberating memory: Our work and our working-class consciousness.* New Brunswick, NJ: Rutgers University Press.

Index